From Mountains High

CONTEMPORARY CATHOLIC MUSIC 1970 - 1985

2018
To Clare —
Christ's peace,
Kim Cardew

From Mountains High
CONTEMPORARY CATHOLIC MUSIC 1970 - 1985

by

Ken Canedo

Foreword by

Dr. Elaine Rendler-McQueeney

Pastoral Press

Portland, Oregon

From Mountains High: Contemporary Catholic Music *1970 - 1985*
Ken Canedo

ISBN 978-1-56929-093-4

© 2018 Pastoral Press
All rights reserved.
An imprint of OCP
5536 NE Hassalo Street
Portland, OR 97213-3638
Phone: 1-800-LITURGY (548-8749)
E-mail: liturgy@ocp.org
web: ocp.org

Publisher: Wade Wisler
Director of Editorial Processes: John Vogler
Worship Publications Manager: Dr. Glenn CJ Byer
Project Editors: Bari Colombari, Jon DeBellis, Aage Nielsen
Cover Design and Book Layout: Stephanie Bozanich
Art Direction: Judy Urben

Printed in the United States of America
ST:0518

Contents

Acknowledgments

The problem with writing a book is that as soon as it hits the shelves, people ask, "When is your next book coming out?" This is especially true of a book on recent history, which, in many ways, is a never-ending story. I knew from the get-go that *Keep the Fire Burning* was only the beginning of the story of contemporary Catholic music. In that book I wrote about songs that are generally not used at liturgy any more, by composers who are either no longer with us or not currently involved in music ministry.

In contrast, the music I chronicle in *From Mountains High* is still very much sung in parishes today, and many of the composers continue to write songs and provide leadership in their communities. This is a living history on a unique art form in which Catholics believe their living Lord is in their midst as they gather together in his name. I can only hope and pray that I have told the story with integrity and compassion.

I am especially grateful to the composers who so generously shared their stories: Carey Landry, Carol Jean Kinghorn-Landry, Dan Schutte, John Foley, SJ, Bob Dufford, SJ, Roc O'Connor, SJ, Tim Manion, Mary Frances Reza, Pedro Rubalcava, Rudy López, Gregory Norbet, John Michael Talbot, Gary Ault, Gary Daigle, Bob Fabing, SJ, Tom Kendzia, Michael Joncas, Bob Hurd, Marty Haugen, and David Haas. Thanks also to former OCP staffers Marie Philippi and Dave Island; to former NALR staffers Erich Sylvester and Robert Lesinski; and to Bruce Bruno, whose stories of his father, Ray Bruno, are an integral part of this book. I also thank Father Virgil Funk, whose work as founder of the National Association of Pastoral Musicians was a turning point for Catholic music ministry in the United States.

I am grateful to John Limb, retired Publisher of OCP, and Wade Wisler, current Publisher, for their encouragement and support; to Vic Cozzoli, retired Chief Products Officer of OCP, whose gentle nudging finally got me started in research and writing; to Bari Colombari, retired Pastoral Press editor who originally sponsored this book, and Jon DeBellis, current managing editor, plus Dr. Glenn CJ Byer, OCP's Worship Publications Manager, who advocated for this book on my behalf and encouraged me to finally get the writing done. Special thanks to the inspiring Dr. Elaine Rendler-McQueeney for writing the Foreword.

Thanks also to Joe Griffith and Kevin Ward for their moral support during my years of writing; to my brother Orlando Canedo, who put up with piles of books strewn all over the house, and to Bruce Hauge, whose personal collection of liturgical LP records was an amazing resource. Lastly, I thank Phillip J. Signey, my friend and classmate from high school and college, who served as my sounding board and grammar guru.

This is a book about music, which cannot be adequately presented by the written word alone. In *Keep the Fire Burning,* copyright law allowed me to share recordings of the pre-1975 music of the Folk Mass era on my website, www.kencanedo.com. This fair use sharing is not permissible for music released after 1975. Happily, the music in *From Mountains High* is available for listening on YouTube and on such streaming services as Apple Music and Spotify. I encourage readers to take advantage of these resources and listen to the contemporary Catholic music of the 1970s and 80s, recorded by the composers themselves.

Foreword

By Dr. Elaine Rendler-McQueeney

In Chapter 1 of Luke's Gospel, the author writes: "So many others have tried their hand at putting together a story of the wonderful harvest of Scripture and history that took place among us, using reports handed down by the original eyewitnesses who served this Word with their very lives. Since I have investigated all the reports in close detail, starting from the story's beginning, I decided to write it all out for you…" (*The Message:* Luke 1:1-4).

This seems suitable for an introduction to Ken Canedo, and the task of documenting the evolution of musical liturgy in the United States since the Second Vatican Council. A sequel to his *Keep the Fire Burning, From Mountains High* takes up where the first book left off.

Ken's new book is a documentary. If art is a reflection of the culture, we must explore what was happening in the world and the Church, to explain how and why this music caught fire and has endured. Ken makes each chapter seem like a fireside chat with a publisher, composer, or storyteller.

Not unlike "temporary altars," many thought folk music would eventually disappear. Much of it did, but as you will read in *From Mountains High,* the movement transitioned from texts best suited for religious education for children, to putting Scripture into the hands of worshippers in song, and in the vernacular. Victorian devotional texts were replaced with biblical texts, and Catholics were exposed to the Bible in a big way! We moved from merely singing about liturgy, to singing the liturgy itself, and from European translations to our American vernacular.

From Mountains High continues with similar, though different, influences on liturgical composition. After folk music, in the secular culture, people were captivated by popular music like The Beatles, who utilized modes, Eastern scales, and unusual instruments—all of which influenced the next part of the Church music story and our culture.

The St. Louis Jesuits introduced us to biblical texts with harmonies that sounded "Catholic" to our ears. Influenced by his classical background, Gregory Norbet introduced an oboe into his music. Catholics fell in love with Black Church music because it was, and is, the authentic expression of a living faith. The Hispanic community exploded with its own rhythms and melodies. Latino, Caribbean, Filipino, and Vietnamese composers embedded texts in the scales and rhythms of each particular culture. Not only does the story continue, it expands to include the scalar forms and idiomatic rhythms of a global Church.

Ken has approached these immediate post-Vatican II years from his perspective as a guitarist and composer. Readers will enjoy learning about the lives of the composers and the stories of their music, and hopefully be inspired to continue to tell their stories in order to nurture a future generation.

Spiritan Father Lucien Deiss, French composer and biblical scholar, once pointed out how every generation of Christians has left its own artistic legacy regarding what Jesus Christ meant to them. We are obligated by tradition to do the same. The Baroque era took 200 years to form. We are only in the first 60 years! Ken Canedo has "investigated all the reports of other eyewitnesses in close detail." May Ken continue his research, and may his work inspire others to document this great time of freedom and creativity, innocence and wisdom, perseverance, and blessing.

Introduction

"The Way We Were"

We are now – in the Me Decade – seeing the upward roll of the third great religious wave in American history.

-Tom Wolfe[1]

Hey, man, have you accepted Jesus Christ as your Lord and Savior?

-Question posed by a Jesus Freak on Hollywood Boulevard

A dawn of hope spreads over the Earth. . . We make no distinction as to race or ideology but seek to secure for the world the dawn of a more serene and joyful day.

-Pope John Paul I[2]

We survived. Somehow, by the grace of God, we survived the 1960s. By 1970, we were drained, shattered, exhausted, and ready to move on. As if on cue, The Beatles called it quits. No one could have written a better epitaph for the turbulent 60s than "Let It Be."

The Candidate was an insightful 1972 movie starring Robert Redford, set during a California senatorial campaign. The incumbent Republican, Senator Crocker Jarmon, was an overwhelming favorite. Democratic organizers, hard-pressed to find a candidate, chose Redford's character, John McKay, simply because he was the son of a former governor.

After a protracted campaign that began with McKay phoning in his appearances, he ended with a more passionate appeal to the voters and won, despite negative polls and predictions. In the memorable final scene, a panicked McKay looked pleadingly into the eyes of his political organizer and asked, "Marvin! What do we do now?"

What indeed would we do now in this bold new decade? To the cynical, Timothy Leary's mantra still resonated: "Turn on, tune in, drop out!" The idealistic turned inward to secular humanist philosophies, EST seminars, and cosmic consciousness. To those who remained within the embrace of organized religion (and they were legion, despite the common impression), the 1970s offered an unparalleled opportunity.

Consider that after years of experimentation, the Second Vatican Council's vernacular liturgy became fully implemented with the 1969 publication of the *Roman Missal*, also known as the *Missal of Pope Paul VI*. The Mass was completely in English (and other lanuages) in the United States, and the introduction of a three-year cycle of Lectionary readings opened up the Scriptures to Catholics like never before. Additional changes in liturgical practice were in store for the new decade, including Communion in the hand and face-to-face Confession.

Consider the sudden growth of the Spanish Mass in America. In 1972, the United States bishops held an unprecedented convocation, *Encuentro Nacional Hispano de Pastoral*. In addition to providing official recognition to the growing Hispanic presence in North America, the *Encuentro* encouraged the promotion of wider participation of Hispanic Catholics in the life and mission of the Church.

Consider how, after a flashy start, the music of the Folk Mass quickly became tired and worn. By 1970, parish folk groups were once again looking to secular sources for their repertoire. One only had to turn on the radio to hear exciting new songs with alleged liturgical possibilities. "My Sweet Lord," "Day by Day," and "Put Your Hand in the Hand" became staples of youth choirs, much to the dismay of many liturgists.

Consider the surprising simultaneous rise of the Jesus Movement and the Charismatic Renewal, two seemingly disparate modern branches of Christianity that were essentially two sides of the same coin: a return to the basic roots of Christ's message, with an emphasis on the dynamic gifts of the Holy Spirit. These movements were producing appealing new songs that would eventually be gathered under the Protestant-oriented umbrella of CCM: Contemporary Christian Music.

In 1972, Bob Dufford, John Foley, Tim Manion, Roc O'Connor, and Dan Schutte were at various stages of their Jesuit formation at Saint Louis University. Utilizing Scripture and the official text of the liturgy as their lyrical source, they composed compelling songs in an uplifting folk style that very quickly caught on around the country. The St. Louis Jesuits became the new standard for Catholic music. Other Catholic artists would emerge in the new decade, including the Monks of Weston Priory, Grayson Warren Brown, and John Michael Talbot.

Decades don't start neatly. So, 1970 still sounded and smelled and looked like the 60s. An unpopular war continued in Vietnam, and draft cards were still being burned. But something was definitely in the air – an intangible assurance that broke through, as a Watergate-ridden White House eventually gave way to a born-again Christian president.

Keep the Fire Burning was the story of the 1960s Folk Mass movement, but its scope ranged from the beginnings of the liturgical movement in the early 20th century through the era of copyright litigation in the late 1970s. *From Mountains High* picks up the story from the end of the Folk Mass period to the beginning of the modern era of Catholic music publishing in 1985. The decades overlap but the story always moves forward.

This is the story of the coming of age of contemporary Catholic music.

---

[1] Fishman, Steve; Homans, John; Moss, Adam, editors, *New York Stories: Landmark Writing from Four Decades of New York Magazine* (New York, NY: Random House, 2008) 452.

[2] Pope John Paul I, *First Address* (to the College of Cardinals at conclusion of Mass in the Sistine Chapel, August 27, 1978), (Washington, DC: United States Catholic Conference, 1979) 7.

Chapter One

"Sing a New Song;" The Founding of NALR

[In the 1960s,] one kind of music absorbed everything else. Now [in the 1970s], the universe of music is expanding on all fronts.

- Clive Barnes, President of Columbia Records[1]

Know well how to give real guidance to the assembly . . . by inspiring the people to sing, by raising the level of their taste, by arousing their desire to take part.

- Pope Paul VI[2]

Looking out the window from his office in downtown Cincinnati, Ray Bruno scratched his dark, short-cropped beard, and realized that it was a mistake to come to work. On April 4, 1974, the newspapers and radio were full of dire warnings and threats of doom: "Severe Weather Watch!" "Storm of the Century Is Coming!" "Shelter at Home!" Bruno, like many downtown workers, dismissed the headlines as mere hype. There was just too much work to do at his fledgling publishing house, North American Liturgy Resources.

The distance between downtown and the Bruno home was 11 miles – a routine 20-minute drive. But this afternoon was anything but routine, and Ray could barely hold himself up as he walked against the howling wind toward his green Mercury Marquis. But now he would have to navigate through the tornado's awesome sway.

His regular route, US-50, was bumper-to-bumper with other frantic commuters. Bruno, a longtime Cincinnati resident, knew his town well, and he opted to take surface streets home. But those streets became a deadly obstacle course of downed telephone lines, severed tree branches, and flying debris.

And then it happened. That fearsome tornado scooped up Bruno's car and tossed him around like an amusement park ride. The car was suddenly airborne, and he gripped the steering wheel, praying for a safe outcome. After landing with a jerky thud, Ray quickly abandoned the now powerless vehicle, and edged his way along front yard fences, dodging playground swing sets, bicycles, and even an above-ground Doughboy swimming pool! He looked up and realized he was miraculously only a few blocks from home. But against this fierce storm, he may as well have been several miles away.

Coming at last to the front door of his house, he fumbled for his keys, even as the door swung open wildly. Disheveled and soaking wet, Ray fell into the welcoming embrace of his wife Shirley, and his children Bruce, Mark, and Beth, who were understandably sick with worry. He gathered the family into the basement, huddling around a transistor radio and listening to updates on the next band of tornadoes.

When it was finally safe to emerge from hiding, Bruno surveyed the extensive neighborhood damage and made a life-changing decision. "We're moving."

"Moving?" said Shirley. "Where to?"

"Any place where there's no wind or tornadoes! Any town where there is no weather!" He scratched his beard thoughtfully. "Let's move to Phoenix!"

· ■ ·

The Bruno family had no connections in Phoenix, Arizona – no relatives, no friends, no one. Ray's son Bruce remembered those days of transition vividly. "We packed our clothing into our green station wagon, and headed for Arizona. We left the house for my mom's mother to pack things up and call the movers in. Dad just wanted out of Cincinnati: for his family, his life, his business. So, he took us to Arizona. Dad was okay with the desert heat. But he was determined to leave the wind and tornadoes behind."[3]

Ray Bruno was born in 1936 in Cincinnati. His parents were Italian immigrants who originally settled in Pittsburgh before moving west to the Queen City. He attended the Franciscan-run Roger Bacon High School and supported his family by working at a local grocery store.

> Dad loved music his whole life. He played sousaphone in his high school's marching band. He also played the accordion and gave lessons. He worked at Pauley's, a big Cincinnati clothing chain. From there he went into the jewelry business. At one time, he managed three jewelry stores simultaneously. And then he met Omer Westendorf at World Library and they became buddies. Dad went to work there as General Manager.[4]

World Library of Sacred Music was a Cincinnati publishing house that wielded enormous influence in the American Catholic Church. While serving as a US soldier in Europe during World War II, Westendorf was impressed by the beautiful music he heard in the churches of Holland and Germany, and struck up deals with European publishers to distribute their choral works in America.

World Library's music became very popular in the States, especially after Westendorf matched the European melodies with modern English texts, resulting in hymnody that was a major step forward from the sentimental devotional Catholic songs of the 1950s. Westendorf collected this music in a hardbound hymnal that he published in 1961: *People's Mass Book*. Westendorf needed a partner with good business sense to manage his growing company. Ray Bruno's experience in retail management complimented Westendorf's background and experience as a church musician.

"In those days, dad did a little bit of everything at World Library. He did the hiring, the selecting of projects, and he supervised the whole process from music development to warehouse."[5]

World Library was an exciting place to work in the 1960s. At the forefront of the burgeoning liturgical scene, the company was involved in record production, music editing, and constant promotion through parish workshops and industry conventions. And then there was Westendorf's colorful side to deal with.

In 1968, when I was very young, I remember being afraid to go into Omer's office because he had a couple of pet baby alligators that he kept in an aquarium near his desk. One Saturday, my brother and I were walking into the building and one of the alligators was loose, walking around! So, Dad jumped out and told us, 'Hang on a second!' He marched into his boss' office and said, 'Omer, can you please put these things away? I've got the kids with me.'[6]

Westendorf's expertise was in choral music, but he had the foresight to appreciate the nascent Folk Mass movement spreading across America. He recognized the potential of Father Clarence Rivers by publishing his *An American Mass Program* in 1963 while the Council Fathers were still deliberating on the *Constitution on the Sacred Liturgy*. Rivers' collection of liturgical music, based on the style of the African American spiritual, was hailed as a breakthrough, and was clearly an act of faith by Westendorf, who had never before published anything other than choral and organ works.

In 1966, Dennis Fitzpatrick's FEL Publications (Friends of the English Liturgy) in Chicago was the acknowledged leader in Folk Mass music. Although World Library did not have a publication as folk-specific as FEL's *Hymnal for Young Christians,* the Cincinnati publisher raised the stakes by including folk hymns in new editions of the *People's Mass Book*. Westendorf even commissioned renowned organist and choral director Jan Vermulst to compose a Mass setting in the folk style, with the self-explanatory title, *Guitar Mass by Jan Vermulst*. He also took care to include guitar chords in the printed music of respected international composer Spiritan Father Lucien Deiss.

Despite World Library's success in the 1960s, by the next decade, the company found itself in a desperate financial situation that required an eventual buyout by the J.S. Paluch Company, an emerging liturgical publisher. In a 1972 letter to FEL's customers, Dennis Fitzpatrick commented:

> It is disheartening to see Mr. Westendorf lose control of the company he founded and through which he contributed so much to worship in the past years. Even more appalling is the realization that a voice of leadership and innovation is effectually stilled in a field that so desperately needs leaders and innovators to produce alternatives for purposeful worship in this country at this time.[7]

Sensing the writing on the wall, Ray Bruno left World Library, and began his own company, Epoch-Universal Publications. He took a handful of folk-based composers with him, including Joe Wise and Carey Landry—a young seminarian from the Diocese of Lafayette, Louisiana, who was studying at The Catholic University of America in Washington, DC.

Starting a new company is a risk, especially in a limited field like liturgical music. To help support his family and cover his payroll, Bruno took on a second job back in the jewelry business and began managing secular music acts to supplement his work with liturgical composers.

Bruce Bruno remembers those days well. "Epoch Records had this band named the Blue Taters, and they sounded like the rock group Chicago. They had a 45 single, 'Stop, Pretty Baby.'"[8]

Blue Taters' popularity in the Cincinnati area more than justified Ray Bruno's strategy of promoting sacred and secular music. He was able to turn his attention to producing Carey Landry's first two albums, *The Spirit Is a-Movin'* and *Great Things Happen*. He also adopted some creative marketing techniques to get the name and products of Epoch-Universal into the public eye. For example, during this time Ray worked with the CBS choir—from the Cincinnati Bible Seminary, not the broadcasting network. He also promoted a young singer-songwriter named Robert Roy.

"Rob Roy. Like the drink. Very familiar sounding," Bruce Bruno recalls with a laugh. "Rob's first album was called *Free*. Dad would call people at stores and say, 'Hey, this is Ray Bruno from Epoch Records and, boy, have I got something for you! I've got the CBS Choir's latest recordings, and I've got the latest album by Rob Roy. It's *Free*."[9]

Rob Roy. The CBS Choir. Epoch Records, whose name on the phone sounded suspiciously like "Epic Records," an affiliate of Columbia Records. This is how Ray Bruno got his foot in the door and attracted people's attention. He even managed to strike up a deal with Decca Records to piggyback on their phenomenally successful rock opera based on the Passion of Christ.

"Dad did everything he could to get the distribution rights for the album *Jesus Christ Superstar*. We were selling the album, and then my dad asked Joe Wise, Carey Landry, and Dan Onley, another seminarian out of Washington, to write a supplementary book, *Jesus Christ Superstar: The Medium and the Message*.[10]

They were trying to tie the secular rock opera to the Church with a study guide. Ray Bruno made sure the cover and graphics of his booklet matched the distinctive brown cover of the popular record, but utilizing a gold face-of-Christ image that implied Decca's twin-angel logo.

This blending of the secular and the liturgical markets was important: "Dad wanted to have the music live on beyond the church," Bruce Bruno recalled. "He wanted people to take it home with them. He wanted to let the people in the pews know: 'This music that you're singing in church today that means so much to you – don't just live church on Sunday. Live church all week! Live it through the music. Take it home with you! Here's a quality recording.'" [11]

In a 1980 profile in *Billboard*, Ray Bruno affirmed his son's recollections. "Our sound is equally as professional as that of secular artists, and our range of styles just as broad.

"The primary interest of a recording company is to produce good music. Our goal is a little more complex. We want to put out the finest sounds for listening *and* for worship. We produce good music with a real good message—one that needs to be heard."[12]

But where did the name "North American Liturgy Resources" come from?

"Epoch-Universal Publications was the original name of dad's company. Because we were doing secular music and sacred music, dad felt like there needed to be a separation. And, particularly since we were doing more sacred as we could afford, he wanted a sacred name. So, it's a literal name: North American Liturgy Resources."[13]

Over the years, as NALR became known as THE publisher of cutting-edge contemporary Catholic music, customers began pronouncing the initials as a noun: "Nailer." The secular productions of Epoch-Universal slowly receded as the liturgical music of NALR grew in popularity. By the time Bruno moved his company to Phoenix after the Cincinnati tornadoes of 1974, Epoch-Universal was retired.

Thus, in the early 1970s NALR was primed and ready to take its place in the annals of contemporary Catholic music.

---

[1] "Mainstream Music Runs Wild," *Our American Century: Time of Transition – The 70s* (Alexandria, VA: Time-Life Books, 1998) 111.

[2] Address to the Tenth International Congress of Church Choirs, 6 April 1970. As quoted in Joncas, Jan Michael, *From Sacred Song to Ritual Music* (Collegeville, MN: The Liturgical Press, 1997) 115.

[3] Interview with the author, February 10, 2007, Beaverton, Oregon.

[4] Ibid.

[5] Ibid.

[6] Ibid.

[7] Fitzpatrick, Dennis, "From the Publisher's Desk," FEL Publications brochure, 1972.

[8] Interview with the author, February 10, 2007, Beaverton, Oregon.

[9] Ibid.

[10] Ibid.

[11] Ibid.

[12] "A Conversation with Raymond P. Bruno," *Billboard,* September 27, 1980.

[13] Interview with the author, February 10, 2007, Beaverton, Oregon.

Keep the Fire Burning: The Story Thus Far

The 1960s was a decade characterized by radical change in just about every field, from politics and race relations to education, science, entertainment, art, morality, and organized religion. The Catholic Church was able to deal with this upheaval because of the Second Vatican Council (1962-1965). Undoubtedly, Catholicism would have survived regardless, as it had for two millennia. But would it have weathered the 60s as well as it did without the Council?

Building on the work of the liturgical movement that emerged in the early 1900s, the Second Vatican Council decreed that the Mass would be translated into the language of the people, who were encouraged to participate in the liturgy like never before. American Catholics, unaccustomed to congregational singing, needed to find their voice in song. In the 1960s, that meant folk music.

To be sure, much of the liturgical innovation in the Catholic Church in the US came about because of the tireless work of liturgists, musicians, and publishers who seized the innovative spirit of Vatican II and took it in directions the Council Fathers never envisioned. The *Constitution on the Sacred Liturgy* spoke highly of Gregorian chant as having "pride of place in liturgical services." The pipe organ was to be "held in high esteem" because it "adds a wonderful splendor to the Church's ceremonies" *(Sacrosanctum Concilium* Nos. 116 and 120). There was no specific mention of folk music and guitars in liturgical music. The document simply spoke of "other instruments" that may be used at Mass. American liturgical innovators took those two words and ran with them. The sound of strumming guitars captured the imagination and energy of many young Catholics, and their participation in the Folk Mass got them involved in their Church.

Our companion book, *Keep the Fire Burning,* told the story of how composers and publishers seized the Folk Mass as their preferred forum for liturgical expression. Publishers such as Omer Westendorf and Dennis Fitzpatrick saw a new liturgical market that was eager to devour any four-chord guitar song – a far cry from the complex choral and organ-oriented works that characterized Catholic publishing before the Council. It was a new paradigm where the sacred and the secular blended in unprecedented ways.

This is the context in which *From Mountains High* begins. Music styles had progressed, and nobody in the 1970s really wanted to sing the songs of the 60s at Mass anymore. Copyright structures were being put in place to ensure just compensation for liturgical composers, who were finally beginning to receive official Church guidelines for their craft. American Catholics were eager for something new. As we saw in the previous decade, this new music would be influenced both by liturgical need and by secular influences that, at first glance, seemed to have no bearing at all with the liturgy. Once again, the sacred and the secular blended.

Chapter Two

"American Pie"
The Culture of the 70s

Here Man completed his first exploration of the Moon, December 1972
A.D. May the spirit of peace in which we came be reflected in the lives
of all mankind.

> -Plaque left on the Moon by the astronauts of Apollo 17,
> the final manned lunar mission

My fellow Americans, our long national nightmare is over.

> -President Gerald R. Ford
> at his inauguration on August 9, 1974

I just believe in me.

> -John Lennon, from his song "God"

It was humanity's grandest and most ambitious adventure, played out on the global stage. When President John F. Kennedy declared in 1961 that by decade's end America would put a man on the moon and return him home safely, he launched an era of space exploration that seized the world's imagination. From John Glenn's riveting triple orbit of Earth in the Mercury capsule, to the euphoria of Apollo 8's Christmas Eve greeting from lunar orbit as the astronauts did a televised reading of the creation story from Genesis—each act in this space drama topped the previous one and kept us enthralled.

On July 20, 1969, Apollo 11 astronaut Neil Armstrong set foot on the moon and declared, "That's one small step for man; one giant leap for mankind." Mission accomplished! And then, America's interests turned elsewhere. Apollo 17 in December of 1972 was the final manned lunar mission to date. The space race came to an abrupt and quiet halt.

In the midst of Cold War vigilance against Communist aggression, President Kennedy sent military advisors to South Vietnam in 1962. When Richard Nixon became president in 1968, he inherited a full-scale military operation in Southeast Asia that already resulted in tens of thousands of US soldiers killed. President Nixon sent special envoy Henry Kissinger to Paris to negotiate "peace with honor." To influence the negotiations, Nixon authorized heavy bombing of Hanoi. The American people were deeply divided over this "undeclared" war.

Popular music reflected the unrest of the people. Pete Seeger was famously banned by the CBS television network from singing "Waist Deep in the Big Muddy" on the

Smothers Brothers Comedy Hour. Crosby, Stills, Nash & Young's protest song, "Ohio," was banned by many AM radio stations because of its anti-Nixon commentary on the National Guard shooting of Kent State students. And "I Feel Like I'm Fixin' to Die Rag" by Country Joe & the Fish became an anti-war rallying chant after the band performed the song at the 1969 Woodstock rock festival.

When the United States finally withdrew its forces on March 29, 1973, about 58,200 US troops had died, including 47,434 in combat. Around 303,660 Americans were wounded, 766 were captured, and more than 2,338 went missing.[1] South Vietnam suffered 313,000 troop deaths with 502,400 wounded.[2] North Vietnamese and Viet Cong troop deaths totaled about 950,756.[3]

There were no victory parades or "mission accomplished" speeches. After all, what was accomplished? President Nixon wanted to send more troops back to Vietnam but he was curtailed by a war-weary Congress and a scandal of his own creation: the Watergate break-in. Here was a president who, in 1972, enjoyed the largest landslide victory in American history, and yet he felt a need to ensure his electoral success through illegal means.

Although the White House disavowed any knowledge of the break-in, investigative reporting by Bob Woodward and Carl Bernstein of the *Washington Post* uncovered a chain of command that reached into the upper echelon of the Nixon administration. Nixon himself consistently denied any wrongdoing, declaring "I am not a crook!" The strategy unraveled when a top aide revealed under Congressional subpoena that Nixon, for historical purposes, tape-recorded every conversation that took place in the Oval Office. Finally, under increasing legal threat, Nixon had no choice but to release the tapes. As members of the House of Representatives began the process for impeachment, the tapes revealed that Nixon had authorized the Watergate cover-up as early as June 23, 1972—six days after the break-in. Faced with clear evidence of obstruction of justice, Nixon resigned the presidency on August 9, 1974.

After more than a decade of war in Vietnam and two years of Watergate, America was torn apart. When Gerald R. Ford was sworn in as president just hours after Nixon stepped down, one could almost hear the American people's collective sigh of relief when Ford declared in his brief inaugural address, "Our long national nightmare is over."[4]

Music of the Seventies

Popular music is a mirror of its times, and the music of the 1970s is no exception, but it had a hard act to follow. The music of the 1960s was alive with a brilliance that swept through the decade as folk music became hit radio and rock'n'roll became rock. When folk music receded in popularity, its message of social awareness merged with rock music, often with dazzling results. Folk troubadour Bob Dylan famously went electric at the Newport Folk Festival in 1965, and the Byrds epitomized the folk-rock movement. There was a blending and appreciation of genres that went across racial lines. White kids and black kids loved the music of Motown, a record label from Detroit that featured The Supremes, The Temptations, and other popular black artists whose smooth soul sound offered an ironic anchor to the struggle for civil rights led by the Rev. Dr. Martin Luther King, Jr. Meanwhile, Jimi Hendrix, a brilliant African American guitarist, was influencing the direction of the white-dominated hard rock scene with records that would come to define the psychedelic acid rock movement. And, as the war in Vietnam imploded into a deadly downward spiral, The Beatles sang "All You Need Is Love."

Oh, those 60s! How could the 70s ever hope to follow such a decade? As if on cue, the 60s music scene disintegrated. Jimi Hendrix and Janis Joplin died of drug overdoses in 1969, just weeks apart from each other. Simon & Garfunkel ended their partnership after one final brilliant album, *Bridge Over Troubled Water*. Perhaps most symbolically, The Beatles broke up. The group who so captivated the world and epitomized the spirit of the 60s sang "Let It Be." Their magical mystery tour was over.

In short, the 70s did not have to worry, because the outgoing decade essentially gave the new decade a clean slate on which to write its own unique music. The former Beatles pointed the way. Their early solo albums were a fascinating window into the individual self-searching that eventually tore them apart. Paul McCartney sang of home-spun domestic bliss in *McCartney*. John Lennon bared his tortured soul in his raw but brilliant *Plastic Ono Band*. George Harrison, who began his journey into Eastern mysticism during The Beatles' middle years, exploded onto the scene with his three-record *All Things Must Pass* that influenced the Jesus rock of the 70s (more of this in Chapter Three). And Ringo Starr created pop music for the sake of pop music in his breezy *Ringo*. It was the individual artist who mattered, not the group.

Indeed, the early 70s saw the emergence of a new trend in singer-songwriters who, arising out of the folk music world of the 60s, captivated music fans with albums that featured a compelling and intimate sound. The troubadours of the new decade included Carole King, James Taylor, Gordon Lightfoot, and Joni Mitchell. Each artist had a unique way of expressing personal and revealing lyrics wrapped in a blend of folk, country, or soft-rock.

> You've got to get up every morning with a smile on your face,
>
> And show the world all the love in your heart…
>
> You're gonna find, yes, you will,
>
> that you're beautiful as you feel.
>
>   -"Beautiful" by Carole King

> I am on a lonely road and I am traveling,
>
> looking for the key to set me free.
>
>   -"All I Want" by Joni Mitchell

Music historian Steve Milward commented on this music trend:

> What unites [singer-songwriters] is the overwhelming impulse to look inward at personal, often private, experiences rather than outward at the issues of the day. Naturally, each songwriter employs his or her own methods. All of them convey their specific message direct to the listener in a way that is often labeled 'confessional.'[5]

To be sure, the music of the 70s was more than the singer-songwriters. Rock groups were still going strong. Bands like Led Zeppelin, and Emerson, Lake & Palmer showcased amazing musicianship that raised the bar in performance quality. Pop music was cranking out radio hits by Carlos Santana, Freddy Fender, The Jackson 5, and more.

Perhaps the self-absorbed preoccupation of the singer-songwriters reached its apex with disco, the dance-based music style of the mid-1970s that emerged from New York's varied subcultures. Slick and studio-generated, with production values that replaced hard-rock guitar solos with sweet synthesizers, disco was anchored by a hypnotic bass drum that thumped the four-beat measures of a dance song like a droning metronome. Skillful disc jockeys kept that beat going in the clubs, and anyone with good moves and sharp clothes could be a star on the dance floor.

Writer Nik Cohn's semi-fictional account of Brooklyn's disco scene caught the eye of Hollywood producer Robert Stigwood, who transformed the story into the fabulously successful movie *Saturday Night Fever* starring John Travolta. When the Bee Gees were brought on board to compose the soundtrack, a national craze was born.

Lyrically, disco is accused of having little or no substance, and the three-word titles of the big disco hits pretty much summarize what the songs were about: "Shake Your Booty," "Get Down Tonight," "Fly, Robin, Fly," "Do the Hustle," and so on. Nevertheless, disco came to epitomize the self-absorbed 1970s. It came as no surprise that at the height of disco's popularity, punk rock flared up with an anarchy-laced explosion as artists like Patti Smith, the Ramones, the Sex Pistols, and X railed against the corporate establishment that had, among other things, taken over the music business.

Hindsight helps us see connections that may not have been initially noticed by those in the midst of a decade's movements and changes. Was narcissism the hallmark of the 70s?

---

[1] National Archives, www.archives.gov

[2] Rummel, R.J., "Vietnam Democide: Estimates, Sources, and Calculations" http://www.hawaii.edu/powerkills/SOD.TAB6.1A.GIF

[3] US Dept. of Defense, "Population and Development Review," Volume 21, Issue 4, p. 790.

[4] For more detailed information on the Watergate scandal and its aftermath, see: Bernstein, Carl, *All the President's Men (1974);* Woodward, Bob, *The Final Days (1976);* Werth, Barry, *31 Days: Gerald Ford, The Nixon Pardon, and a Government in Crisis* (New York, Anchor Books, 2006).

[5] Milward, Steve, *Different Tracks: Music and Politics in 1970* (Leicestershire, UK: Matador®, 2014).

The Self-Esteem Movement

It came about so gradually and blossomed with such subtlety that hardly anybody noticed when self-esteem became a "movement." Psychologist Nathaniel Brandon, often cited as a prime influence because of his 1969 book, *The Psychology of Self-Esteem*, argued that "feelings of self-esteem were the key to success in life." Brandon's concepts seized the public's imagination, and influenced such diverse fields as counseling, entertainment, and even religion. But self-esteem would have its most lasting influence in the field of education, as principals, teachers, school boards, textbook writers, and television programmers (e.g., *Sesame Street*) used self-esteem as the foundation for the modern learning experience. Among the principal points of a self-esteem program are a healthy confidence in one's abilities, trusting one's judgment, not worrying excessively about the past or the future, and a sensitivity to the needs of others.

Self-esteem in education had its heyday in the 70s, but the backlash today is considerable. Paul C. Vitz, longtime professor of psychology at New York University, delivered the following observation to an audience of priests in New Westminster, British Columbia, Canada, in 1995.

> Self-worth, a feeling of respect and confidence in one's being, has merit. But an ego-centered, let me feel good self-esteem, where we can ignore our failures and our need for God is quite another thing. What is wrong with the concept of self-esteem? The bottom line is that no agreed upon definition or measure for self-esteem exists. And whatever self-esteem is, no reliable evidence supports self-esteem scores as meaning much at all.[1]

The self-esteem movement permeated popular culture. Dr. Jean M. Twenge, a noted Generation X psychologist, observed how the self-esteem movement affected the Baby Boom generation.

> In contrast to the previous [generation's] ethics of honor and duty, Baby Boomer ideals focused instead on meaning and self-fulfillment. In his 1976 bestseller, *Your Erroneous Zones,* Wayne Dyer suggests that the popular song "You Are the Sunshine of My Life" be retitled "I AM the Sunshine of My Life." Your love for yourself, he says, should be your "first love." The 1970 allegory, *Jonathan Livingston Seagull,* describes a bird bored with going "from shore to shore and back again." Instead, he wants to enjoy flying, swooping through the air to follow "a higher meaning, a higher purpose for life," even though his actions get him exiled from his flock. The book, originally rejected by nearly every major publishing house, became a runaway bestseller as Americans came to agree with the idea that life should be fulfilling and focused on the needs of the self. The seagulls in the animated movie *Finding Nemo* were still on message almost twenty-five years later: all that comes out of their beaks is the word "Mine."[2]

A full in-depth treatment of the self-esteem movement is beyond the scope of this book. The purpose of citing it here is to point out its importance as one of the forces of the 1970s that influenced Catholic songwriting for the liturgy.

---

[1] Catholic Education Resource Center website: http://www.catholiceducation.org/en/education/catholic-contributions/the-problem-with-self-esteem.html

[2] Twenge, Jean M., *Generation Me: Why Today's Young Americans Are More Confident, Assertive, Entitled — and More Miserable Than Ever Before* (New York: Free Press, 2006) 45-46.

Chapter Three

"Put Your Hand in the Hand"
The Jesus and Charismatic Movements
Jesus on the Radio

Something new and strange has hit the current religious scene in America, and most observers are baffled by it. Hippies and drug addicts are becoming Christians in significant numbers. The new Christians are known variously as Jesus Freaks, Jesus People, Street Christians; there is talk of a Jesus Movement, or a Jesus Revolution.[1]

-Ronald M. Enroth, Edward Ericson,
and C. Peters, authors of *The Jesus People*

The renewal did not go away, as many had hoped, and as some unrealistically expect. It continues to be an instrument of radical religious conversion in the lives of thousands of Catholics, for many of whom it has become their most important link to Jesus and to the church.[2]

-Father John B. Healey

Take a look, open your eyes.
He'll show it to you.

-John Fischer, from his song "Jesus, My Lord"[3]

Suddenly, in the early 1970s, they were everywhere. In the seedy part of Hollywood Boulevard in Los Angeles, a smiling long-haired young man would give you a copy of the *Hollywood Free Paper* while asking, "Have you accepted Jesus Christ as your Lord and Savior?" In the Haight-Ashbury district in San Francisco, hippies were chanting, "We are one in the Spirit, we are one in the Lord." At Seattle's Pike Place Market, a sincere young woman might place a pamphlet in your hand, inviting you to a nearby prayer meeting.

> I remember you. You were baptized one summer afternoon in the warm, sparkling surf at Corona del Mar, or maybe in the chilly waters of Woody Island in Kodiak, Alaska. You stood on a noisy, traffic-clogged street corner in Los Angeles, Detroit, Kansas City, Minneapolis or Cleveland handing out copies of the *Hollywood Free Paper* to everyone who passed by.
>
> We met at a "jeans and T-shirts" Bible study at Calvary Chapel in Costa Mesa, or was it the House of Joshua in Coeur d'Alene, Idaho? I saw you at a Jesus rap in that rambling, two-story Green Pastures house in Pomona, or maybe we prayed together in the cozy House of Manna in Port Angeles, Washington.[4]

Yes, the Jesus People were everywhere, and they took the media and organized religion by surprise. Near-simultaneous cover stories featured the movement in *Time, US News & World Report, Look* and *Life* magazines. What exactly was the Jesus movement? Ronald M. Enroth, Edward E. Ericson, Jr., and C. Breckenridge Peters offer a salient summary in their 1972 book: *The Jesus People: Old-Time Religion in the Age of Aquarius.*

> The Jesus movement is characterized by certain basic tenets held by most or all of its members: insistence on the simplicity of the gospel, a sense of the impending end of the world, espousal of charismatic gifts, and efforts to achieve a sense of community.[5]

The *Hollywood Free Paper* was a popular nationally distributed newssheet of the Jesus movement based in Los Angeles. William Kimball, a contributing writer, eloquently remembered his days as a young participant in the movement.

> We were as spiritually ignorant and deceived as they came. We had done it all: drugs, sex, rock & roll, protests, occult, astrology, witchcraft, New Age, eastern religions, TM [transcendental meditation], gurus, even health foods, but nothing had filled the emptiness in our soul until we met Jesus. Simply put, it was a time when Jesus really was our first love.

> In reality, the established church had almost nothing to do with this sovereign move of God on a counter-culture that had, for all intents and purposes, been "written off" by them.[6]

As with any organic movement, the memories of its origin vary from storyteller to storyteller. Lonnie Frisbee, a leading Jesus Freak from the Bay Area, suggested that the foundation of the movement was the Six-Day War in June 1967 between Israel and the Arab nations that surrounded it. Israel regained its territory, and that was a sign of the end times, preceded by a great outpouring of the Holy Spirit.

Synergistically, 1967's Summer of Love attracted scores of young people from across America to San Francisco's Haight-Ashbury district, which became fertile ground for street preachers. Ted Wise, a Christian from nearby Sausalito, befriended lost young people who had nothing better to do that summer. He gave personal witness that Jesus was a much holier high than any drug, and he soon had a sizeable following. This led to the opening of a storefront coffee house christened The Living Room. Suddenly, Jesus was cool in a way that these young people had never experienced before in the Sunday schools of their childhood. The Living Room reportedly ministered to 50,000 young seekers during its two-year heyday.

The numbers continued to grow, and Wise established a community at a farmhouse in Novato, north of San Francisco. This "Christian commune" was eventually called the House of Acts. Lonnie Frisbee and several other future leaders of the Jesus movement joined Wise's community which eventually dispersed to Ohio, New York, Palo Alto and, most significantly, Southern California, where Frisbee became youth minister at Calvary Chapel in Costa Mesa.[7]

The Charismatic Renewal seemed to happen almost simultaneously with the Jesus movement. Indeed, one could make an argument that the Charismatic Renewal was organized religion's "adoption" of the Jesus movement into its denominational ranks. That is an oversimplification, but there are areas of overlap. The Charismatic Renewal traces its roots to the American Pentecostal movement of the early 19th century during the so-called Great Awakening, when the Quakers, Shakers, Irvingites, Mormons, and other groups preached that external manifestations were an essential part of Christian belief. The Holiness movement, an offshoot of the Methodist church, was a forerunner to the Pentecostal movement.

> Ideologically, the Holiness people claimed that justification is followed by a special blessing which is distinct from conversion; that the blessing is to be sought and can be obtained through such collective outbursts of fervor as revivals might produce; and sanctified Christians should forsake the world and its sinful allurements.[8]

In 1900, Charles Fox Parham, a white preacher, established an early Pentecostal congregation in Kansas City that was renowned for its faith healings. His disciple, William J. Seymour, a black preacher, migrated to Los Angeles and established the Azusa Street Revival, attracting large crowds from the African-American community as Pentecostalism spread out into a worldwide movement. These congregations were characterized by their feverish services that featured fiery preaching, faith healings, and praying in tongues, a literal interpretation of 1 Corinthians chapters 12–14 in which Saint Paul speaks of the spiritual gifts.

Pentecostal congregations flourished for many years as a unique branch of Protestantism but entered the mainstream when their distinctive worship experience was adopted by some mainline churches in the late 1950s. Lutherans in Minnesota and Episcopalians in California felt called by the Holy Spirit to begin praying in tongues. The renewal's entry into Catholicism soon followed.

> The roots of the movement are buried in a 1967 student-faculty retreat at Duquesne University [a Catholic college] in Pittsburgh. The retreat had been preceded by a deep concern of a few people over personal spiritual stagnation and powerlessness; many participants had been impressed by the influence of Protestant charismatics who had led retreat leader Ralph Kiefer into the Pentecostal experience known as the baptism in the Spirit. During the weekend, a Pentecostal-style revival—complete with speaking in tongues—took place.

> News of the retreat spread to Notre Dame, where students and faculty members launched a similar group with the aid of local Protestant charismatics. From Notre Dame, the revival movement spread.[9]

Needless to say, the sudden entrance of charismatic prayer into the Catholic Church raised concern among pastors and the hierarchy. On the plus side, the renewal was contributing to an upswing in new members and a revitalized prayer life in the parish. Thoughtful bishops appointed theologians to oversee the movement in their dioceses.

Jesuit Father Ralph Tichenor served in this capacity in the Archdiocese of Los Angeles, and Cardinal Leon Suenens, Archbishop of Mechelen-Brussels, advised Pope Paul VI on the renewal. These advisors worked hard to bring sound theology and Catholic teaching to the renewal. As an example, here is Father Tichenor's response to a question about the gift of tongues.

> Some non-Catholic groups who do not have a sacramental understanding of the Church use the gift of tongues as a visible sign of unity with the Spirit. Catholics, however, believe that the Spirit comes through the sacraments, especially Baptism.

> On the other hand, I do believe that the Holy Spirit is pouring out the charismatic gifts — including the gift of tongues — on all Catholics just as during the infancy of the Church.[10]

The Charismatic Renewal appealed to the multicultural nature of the Catholic Church as the charismatic gifts and emotional style of worship were not exclusive to the English-speaking.

> Many come from more expressive cultures of worship and feel more at home with their hands in the air, shouting in tongues at a prayer meeting, than they do in a traditional Irish or Italian Catholic parish (the appeal of charismatic renewal in the Global South – Africa, Latin America, and developing Asia — was never lost on authorities in Rome).[11]

As the Jesus movement and Charismatic Renewal took root in America, Jesus was all over the airwaves. The Edwin Hawkins Singers won a Grammy in 1970 for their arrangement of the spiritual, "Oh, Happy Day," and that was soon followed on the charts with Judy Collins' version of "Amazing Grace," and "Spirit in the Sky" by Norman Greenbaum. The year 1971 brought "Think His Name" by Johnny Rivers, "Put Your Hand in the Hand" by Ocean, and the phenomenal international Number One hit, "My Sweet Lord" by former Beatle, George Harrison. In 1972, we could turn on the radio and hear the Gaelic hymn "Morning Has Broken" by Cat Stevens, "Jesus is Just Alright" by the Doobie Brothers, and the appealing "Day by Day," a show-stopping number from the popular Broadway musical, *Godspell*.[12]

There were two major musicals about Jesus. The first one, *Jesus Christ Superstar* by Andrew Lloyd Webber and Tim Rice, was released as a double-LP record on October 27, 1970. The album and subsequent live productions and film were controversial from the start. They portrayed Jesus not as God, but as a very human revolutionary who fell victim to the cascading events that led to his crucifixion. Set in the final week of Jesus' life, the lyrics and story took great liberty with the Gospel narratives, emphasizing the character interplay between the Passion story's main players and the political conflict between the Romans and the Jews of first century Palestine.

Lloyd Webber's stunning musical score was a grand mixture of rock and pop styles, augmented by a full orchestra. The rock nature of the opera served to underscore the portrayal of Jesus and his Apostles as countercultural hippies. Indeed, Rice's lyrics mixed then-current slang and modern allusions with ancient biblical imagery. Conservative Christian groups were offended, and they criticized the show's lack of a resurrection scene along with its sympathetic treatment of Judas. The BBC originally banned the album as sacrilegious. But all the controversy only served to push the work's popularity as *Jesus Christ Superstar* became the top-selling album of 1971 on the US Billboard Pop chart.

"We tried to bring him down from the stained-glass windows," said Lloyd Webber. Lyricist Tim Rice further expanded on his intent. "Basically, the idea of our whole opera is to have Christ seen through the eyes of Judas. While we don't see him as God, the opera doesn't categorically say he wasn't. The question is left open."[13]

Godspell's light comical tone stood in marked counterpoint to the somberness of *Jesus Christ Superstar*. While *Superstar* was only loosely based on the Passion accounts, the script for *Godspell* was unabashedly centered around Jesus' parables, mostly from the Gospel of Matthew.

That synopsis makes this musical seem innocent enough, but what made *Godspell* so endearing—and controversial—was the way Jesus and his disciples were dressed as "flower children" clowns, singing and dancing their way through the parables with brilliant catchy pop songs by Stephen Schwartz, who took his lyrics directly from the Episcopal hymnal. Churches everywhere soon took cues from this musical, encouraging their teens to create parable skits on youth night, and singing the joyful *Godspell* songs at Sunday services. The play may have also influenced the growth in a catechetical approach known as "clown ministry." But, like its rock opera predecessor, *Godspell* has no direct resurrection scene. Composer Schwartz commented on this in the official script.

> Over the years, there has been comment from some about the lack of an apparent resurrection in the show. Some choose to view the curtain call, in which Jesus appears, as symbolic of the resurrection; others point to the moment when the cast raise Jesus above their heads. While either view is valid, both miss the point. *Godspell* is about the formation of a community which carries on Jesus' teachings after he has gone. In other words, it is the effect Jesus has on the other which is the story of the show, not whether or not he himself is resurrected.[14]

Godspell continues to be performed to this day, including a *Godspell Junior* edition that is a favorite of middle-school drama clubs. Despite the heated polemics—or perhaps because of it—both *Godspell* and *Jesus Christ Superstar* were part of the "perfect storm" of 1970s pop culture events that pointed to the overall Jesus movement.

Also on the radio was a rock-flavored version of the Our Father. "The Lord's Prayer," as sung by Australian Sister Janet Mead, was a certified gold record that sold more than 1 million copies in 1974. Janet Mead was a talented singer who, at age 17, formed a music group called The Rock Band specifically to sing for Mass at the local cathedral in Adelaide. She joined the Sisters of Mercy and began teaching music at two Catholic schools.

Her work with using rock music to inspire Catholic youth caught the attention of Martin Erdman, a noted producer in Sydney who recorded Sister Janet singing a cover of Donovan's "Brother Sun, Sister Moon," the theme song from Franco Zeffirelli's 1973 film on the life of Saint Francis of Assisi. As an afterthought, they recorded Sister Janet singing the Lord's Prayer setting that was composed by Arnold Strais, a friend and musician from her parish. Erdman's record label released it as a single. To everyone's delightful surprise, it became a #3 hit in Australia. A&M Records got wind of the single and released it in America, where it reached an impressive #4 on the Billboard charts. The record has the distinction of being the only Top 10 hit whose lyrics were attributed to Jesus Christ.[15]

The secular Jesus music of the early 70s influenced future Christian songwriters on the possibilities of merging popular music styles with sacred texts and themes. John Fischer, a contemporary Christian singer-songwriter who initially recorded with FEL Publications during the Folk Mass days, reflected on this blending of message and medium.

> I found folk and folk-rock to be a very passionate force in our culture for things beyond just falling in love. There are lots of messages involved: civil rights, the war in Vietnam, and peace, and love, making a new world, and all those things. Well, if we're going to have all that, why not have a spiritual preaching message? Why not have a message of faith?[16]

Contemporary Christian Music (CCM) is a mostly Protestant-based phenomenon that deserves its own book-length treatment. There are a host of record labels and publishers in the multimillion-dollar CCM industry, but it's worth highlighting the origins of at least one major label that was an integral part of the Jesus movement.

Maranatha! Music (yes, with the exclamation point) was founded in 1971 by Chuck Smith, Sr., of Calvary Chapel in Costa Mesa – the same Southern California church that welcomed the Jesus People and made them a central focus of their mission. The charismatic and ingratiating Pastor Smith and his staff welcomed young people in droves, and they packed the church on Sundays and at Wednesday Bible study. Contemporary music played an important role.

> The entire youthful congregation joins in singing "Pass It On" or a similar song that often includes swaying with the music, arms interlocked. Individual soloists perform, accompanied by a guitar, and share music received "from the Spirit." Some of the musical groups – like Country Faith and Blessed Hope – are somewhat more enthusiastically received and enliven the tempo of the evening. As each song ends, members of the audience point their forefinger heavenward in the Christian sign meaning that there is only one way and it is through Jesus Christ.[17]

Baptism services were held at the beach in nearby Corona del Mar, and the outdoor setting showed the effectiveness of this new music. The catchy refrains were easily learned, and these songs spread quickly throughout America. A stellar lineup of music groups and solo artists were performing at Calvary Chapel, including Mustard Seed

Faith, Chuck Girard, and Karen Lafferty (composer of the iconic "Seek Ye First"). Pastor Smith and his advisors soon saw the need to record and publish their home-grown talent, eventually taking on the name Maranatha! Music.

The songs of Maranatha! Music eventually found their way into the Catholic reper-toire, thanks to LifeTeen, a youth ministry program that attracted Catholic teens to deeper involvement in the Church through engaging homilies, full youth involve-ment in liturgical ministries, and rocking contemporary music. Songs like "As the Deer," "Humble Thyself in the Sight of the Lord," "Seek Ye First," "Let the Walls Fall Down," and "Lord, I Lift Your Name On High" were among the many Maranatha! Music songs that became a staple of Catholic youth ministry, and would eventu-ally influence such composers as Tom Booth, Steve Angrisano, Matt Maher, Sarah Hart, Jesse Manibusan, and others who became part of OCP's contemporary division, *Spirit & Song,* in the late 1990s.

But we jump ahead. First, there is a mountain to climb. Several 1970s Catholic com-posers began that journey by heeding the Second Vatican Council's challenge to read the signs of their times.[18]

1   Enroth, Ronald; Ericson, Edward E.; Peters, C. Breckinridge, *Jesus People: Old-Time Religion in the Age of Aquarius* (Grand Rapids, MI: William B. Eerdmans Publishing Company, 1972) 9.
2   Healey, Rev. John B., "Some Questions About Catholic Charismatics," *America* (Jesuit magazine), December 9, 1978, 139:429.
3   "Jesus, My Lord" ©1970, by Songs and Creations, Inc.
4   *Hollywood Free Paper,* http://www.hollywoodfreepaper.org
5   Enroth, Ronald; Ericson, Edward E.; Peters, C. Breckinridge, *Jesus People: Old-Time Religion in the Age of Aquarius* (Grand Rapids, MI: William B. Eerdmans Publishing Company, 1972), back cover.
6   Kimball, William, "We Were Once Called Jesus Freaks," *Hollywood Free Paper,* http://www.hollywoodfreepa-per.org/article.php?id=16
7   Maranatha! Music, an eventual giant in the Contemporary Christian Music industry, had its beginnings at Calvary Chapel. (More on the music later in this chapter.)
8   Hardon, John A., *The Protestant Churches of America* (New York: Image Books, 1969) 170.
9   Plowman, Edward. E., "Catholic Charismatics: An Evangelistic Thrust," *Christianity Today.* September 22, 1978, 22:42.
10 Chervin, Rhonda, *Why I Am a Catholic Charismatic* (Liguori Publications, 1980) 51.
11 Worthen, Molly, "Charismatic Catholicism is alive and well," CRUX, September 26, 2014. http://www.cruxnow.com/faith/2014/09/26/charismatic-catholicism-is-alive-and-well/
12 The secular Christian hits continued as the decade progressed, including "You Light Up My Life" by Debbie Boone" (1977); and Bob Dylan's Christian album *Slow Train Coming* (1978).
13 James, David and Sanders, John, *Jesus Christ Superstar: From the Motion Picture* (Hertfordshire, England: Fountain Press, 1973) 92.
14 stephenschwartz.com
15 "Australian Music & Popular Culture, 1964-1975: Sister Janet Mead" http://www.milesago.com/Artists/janet-mead.htm
16 Phone interview with the author, August 17, 2005, from Encino, California. As cited in Canedo, Ken, *Keep the Fire Burning: The Folk Mass Revolution* (Portland, OR: Pastoral Press, 2009) 94.
17 Enroth, Ronald; Ericson, Edward E.; Peters, C. Breckinridge, *Jesus People: Old-Time Religion in the Age of Aquarius* (Grand Rapids, MI: William B. Eerdmans Publishing Company, 1972) 86-87.
18 *Gaudium et Spes (Pastoral Constitution on the Church in the Modern World, December 7, 1965)* paragraph 4.

Born-Again Christian President

James Earl Carter, known throughout his life as "Jimmy," was the 39th President of the United States, elected in 1977 to serve a single term. Carter had a meteoric political career, rising from peanut farmer to state senator, and then governor of Georgia. He seemed to come out of nowhere in 1976 when he stormed the primaries, secured the Democratic nomination for President, and defeated the incumbent Gerald R. Ford. His victory was viewed as a national mandate for change by Americans who had grown weary of war and Watergate. But it was Carter's personal faith that caught the imagination of voters. He was the first presidential candidate to openly admit that he was a born-again Christian.

On a recent radio interview, Mr. Carter shared how his faith shaped his decision to enter politics and his tenure as President.

> I worship the Prince of Peace, not war. And I felt as a president and as a governor that I should promote the concept of peace. And human rights as an aspect of justice, and alleviation of suffering are in the footsteps of Christ through foreign aid and through treaty. I had some conflicts. The most serious conflict for me, as a president, was concerning abortion.

Catholics, and a growing number of people of all faiths disagree vehemently with these "exceptions," but they can understand President Carter's dilemma:

> I've never approved of abortion, and I don't believe that Christ would approve unlimited abortion. I do have an ability to rationalize that it's OK in the case of rape or incest, or if the mother's life is in danger, but very strict interpretation or limits on abortion.

> I took an oath of office to uphold the Constitution of the United States as interpreted by the Supreme Court, and Roe versus Wade was in effect then. So, I tried to minimize the need for abortion by promoting adoptions and by encouraging young people to know how to avoid unwanted pregnancy. And if a woman did find that she was pregnant, to carry her pregnancy to birth with the full assurance, and this was missing then, and is still missing now, that that when the baby came, that she and the baby would have unlimited health care and support.

> I couldn't overthrow a change in Supreme Court ruling. I had to comply with it. So that was one of the quandaries in which I found myself. And, of course I figured out a way, which all human beings to do, to rationalize what I did. I said, 'I'm enforcing the Supreme Court ruling, but I'm doing the best I can to avoid abortion.'

> We are all saved by the grace of God through our faith in Jesus Christ. And if we believe that, we are Christians, and we should love one another. I think that John's first epistle is an equally expressive and emotional and complete picture of what love ought to be, not only between Christians, but between Christians and other people.[1]

---

[1] "On Being: The Private Faith of Jimmy Carter" Transcript of radio interview, April 26, 2007. http://www.onbeing.org/program/private-faith-jimmy-carter/transcript/1321

Chapter Four

"Hi God!"
Children's Music
NALR Composers

You are a child of the universe, no less than the trees and the stars; you have a right to be here.

-"Desiderata" by Max Ehrmann (1927; popularized by Les Crane in his 1971 hit single)

In addition to expressing texts, music can also unveil a dimension of meaning and feeling, a communication of ideas and intuitions which words alone cannot yield. This dimension is integral to the human personality and to growth in faith. It cannot be ignored if the signs of worship are to speak to the whole person.

-*Music in Catholic Worship*, paragraph 24[1]

In 1968, Carey Landry was a seminarian at The Catholic University of America in Washington, DC, studying for the Diocese of Lafayette in Louisiana. He transferred there from Notre Dame Seminary in New Orleans, where he enjoyed a brief musical partnership with Gary Ault, later of the Dameans. At that time, Notre Dame's liturgies were steeped in chant and choral music. Carey would not experience the new guitar-strummed Folk Mass until he arrived at Catholic University's Theological College.

"That's where I became so enamored of the Folk Mass," Carey remembers. "By then I had learned to play the guitar a little bit, and began participating in the group, and finally, began to lead them."

The weekly Folk Mass at Theological College was open to the general public, and it typically attracted a large crowd of people from around the Washington, DC, region. Musicians and pastoral teams approached Carey, inviting him to their parishes to help establish their own folk liturgies. At one point, the young song leader became involved in five or six parishes a month.

Inspired by Vatican II and the social justice bent of 1960's folk music, Carey's first composition, "The Spirit Is A-Movin'," became an anthem for those idealistic times. Carey began composing in earnest for the liturgy, and his early songs were collected on three seminal albums: *The Spirit Is A-Movin'*, *Yes, Lord*, and *Great Things Happen!* – all released by a fledgling publishing house, North American Liturgy Resources.[2]

In 1973, Ray Bruno believed he could offer something fresh and exciting. He and his staff worked hard to make a name for their company. With Bruno as president, the staff consisted of Dan Onley as director of publications; David Serey as production manager; Erich Sylvester as executive producer of recordings; and a group of notable advisors that included Joe Wise, Dan Creed, Father James Dallen, Ann Onley, and Carey Landry.

Sylvester remembered the dynamics that Bruno and Onley shared. "Ray came from the business world, and Dan had been a seminarian. Dan was the one who had knowledge of liturgy, whereas Ray's liturgical knowledge was minimal and just acquired by working at World Library. That was the original fundamental partnership between them. That chemistry worked for a while. Dan knew Carey Landry. Ray knew Joe Wise. At NALR's beginning, those two artists were the fundamental basis of their success."[3]

Landry's three albums were beginning to get noticed, thanks to his non-stop concert tours and workshop appearances. As one reviewer at the time noted: "Carey's three albums of liturgical songs serve their intended purpose by demonstrating his songs. But Carey performing live is something else again! Powerful, moving, spontaneous, uplifting!"[4]

It was at one of his parish appearances that Landry had a life-changing encounter with a catechist who was creatively using his music for religious education.

Carol Jean Kinghorn grew up in Indianapolis and taught in several schools there. She was concerned about the way children were learning about God. Carol Jean reflected:

> I noticed that children didn't have any understanding of God…except through laws, regulations and catechism questions. That's as far as they knew. It was not on any kind of feeling level. It was just 'I have to answer this question about God or about Jesus.' That troubled me so much. I had a deep faith and prayer life and love for God. I wanted to communicate that to children.
>
> I also loved music, so I began to research what kind of music was out there that can speak to children. The music that we were singing in church didn't really communicate on the level I felt that children needed. So, I began to go to bookstores and music stores to search for music. There was very little out there.

One of Carey's songs, "Only a Shadow," caught the ear of Carol Jean. She taught the song to her first-grade students, who sang along enthusiastically. Carey and Carol Jean met at her parish, Saint Thomas Aquinas Church, when Carey gave a concert there in 1972. Literally bumping into each other on the church grounds before the event, the teacher shared with the songwriter how much children loved his music. From that chance encounter grew a collaboration that would soon transform the role of music in religious education.

"Carol Jean started telling me about what she was doing with my music in her classroom," Carey recalled. "I was absolutely fascinated! We struck up a friendship and I began corresponding with her."

"In our classroom, we did a lot of things," said Carol Jean. "I worked with the children in building community because I knew that anything that could happen in children's lives with God—in their prayer life—had to revolve around community. Carol Jean continues:

> The children would be able to say to one another, 'You hurt me when you did this today and I'd like to give you forgiveness for that.' Then, the other child would say, 'Well, thank you for forgiving me.' We did this every day during 'peace time,' when we shared at a deeper level. We prayed together. It was the children's words. Through these various activities, the children would be able to say how they felt about God, and how they felt about one another, and what love meant to them. The children began to write down their prayers and their thoughts. That's what I sent to Carey.[5]

Carey continued the story:

> Carol Jean would send me the ideas and themes the children were working on. And I would take those themes, write songs, and send them back to her. If the children responded to it then we knew it was good. It was all done through trial and error by having her test the songs with the children. We did our first workshop together in 1972, before *Hi God* had come into existence. We produced a cassette tape in my office of 17 songs for children, and the response to that was absolutely incredible. That's when we knew we had to put *Hi God* out there.

> I would come twice a year and visit the classroom where Carol Jean was teaching. And we would work with the children. We actually worked with her first and second grade classes for the original recordings of *Hi God* and *Hi God 2*. That's why it's not polished.[6]

> And once *Hi God* got published, we were traveling as much as we could. We traveled once a month. I remember one time we were in Kansas City on Friday, Washington, DC, on Saturday, and Philadelphia on Sunday. In one weekend! We just went all over the country, and, ultimately, Australia.[7]

Hi God succeeded because of its winning combination of effective children's music plus creative and relentless marketing. NALR's seasonal newsletter trumpeted Landry's and Kinghorn's achievement:

> HI GOD! is a long-awaited ecumenical program based on the human growth and development of children – and all those who wish to open themselves to love . . .

> HI GOD! is a unique religious education program for all elementary levels . . .

> HI GOD! is a proven and practical approach to letting faith, growth and love, discovery, trust and hope become the foundation for the TOTAL education experience . . .[8]

Hi God reportedly sold $1 million worth of products in its first year and helped put NALR on the map. The basic kit consisted of two stereo LPs, an Idea and Resource Book for teachers, the complete music book for the songs, special posters and other teaching materials in an attractive box. *Hi God* was perfectly timed to meet a big demand in the decade when the self-esteem movement was having an influence in educational circles, especially among school age children.

There were 27 songs in the original *Hi God*. One of them, "His Banner Over Me Is Love," became a beloved classic for an entire generation of Catholic children who remember singing it at their First Communion with fun hand gestures.

> He calls us all to his banqueting table,
> his banner over me is love.

Text: Based on Song of Songs 2:4. Verses 1, 4-5, Carey Landry, ©1975, OCP. All rights reserved.

At this writing, Carey and Carol Jean are in production to release *Hi God 7* with OCP in 2018.

·■·

Flush from the success of *Hi God,* Ray Bruno and his staff continued to grow their company. Along with Landry and Kinghorn, they recruited an impressive group of established and up-and-coming composers.

Joe Wise

The story of Joe Wise, a 70s seminarian and Folk Mass pioneer, was told in *Keep the Fire Burning.*[9] He released a string of popular records on his own Fontaine House label that were distributed by NALR. His 1970 album, *A New Day,* featured "Lord, Teach Us to Pray," a deeply personal composition that struck a chord with many. It is a song of its time.

> Lord, teach us to pray.
> It's been a long and cold December kind of day.
> With our hearts and hands all busy
> in our private little wars,
> we stand and watch each other now
> from separate shores.
> We lose the way.
>
> I need to know today the way things should be in my head.
> I need to know for once now the things that should be said.
> I've got to learn to walk around as if I were not dead.
> I've got to find a way to learn to live.

©1970, 1994, GIA Publications, Inc.

Wise reflected on the origins of this song in his recent memoir, *The Truth in Plenty*:

> This one came in a whoosh. One sitting. At night. With Maleita, my wife, and Michelle, 30, and John, 1, asleep. Alone in the small cubicle of my home office. Words and melody it came, flowing.
>
> Things were not going great for the country. War in Vietnam. A morally shaky White House. Unrest in the streets. Assassinations of our best and brightest. I felt we were losing our way. That's what they called Christianity in the early days, 'the Way.'[10]

Although he maintained recording and publishing independence, Wise gladly served as an advisor to NALR. He ended up recording 22 albums of music—for liturgy, for children, and for his own reflections on life. As the years progressed, he found a non-denominational spiritual path. He has taught writing as a therapeutic tool in treatment centers for addiction, and conducts retreats on journaling as a gateway for spiritual awareness. He now lives with his wife Maleita near Sedona, Arizona.

Neil Blunt and C.P. Mudd

Neil Blunt and C.P. (Pat) Mudd, together with fellow composer Jack Miffleton, were seminarians together at Saint Mary's Seminary in Baltimore, Maryland. Their years together resulted in Miffleton's bestselling World Library album, *With Skins and Steel*.[11] After leaving Saint Mary's, Blunt was involved with the Cincinnati Metropolitan Housing Commission, and eventually became its director. He continued to compose liturgical music.

Blunt also collaborated on a collection of liturgical music with Father C.P. Mudd, who was ordained for the Archdiocese of Louisville. Their album was called *Possible Gospel,* inspired from a line in the title song: "Isn't it the Gospel that says for man it's possible to lead his life in a better way?"

Pat Mudd eventually married, and became executive director of the Arthur S. Kling Center, a not-for-profit neighborhood senior center in the Louisville, Kentucky area. He passed away in 2005.

Bernard Huijbers, S.J.

Bernard Huijbers (1922–2003) studied under Ernest Mulder during his Jesuit course of studies, receiving the state certificate for music theory in 1951. He served as senior master of school music, and choirmaster at Saint Ignatius College, Amsterdam, The Netherlands, until 1969. Afterwards, he served as composer, choir director, and liturgical team member at Saint Dominic's parish in Amsterdam.

Huijbers' work as composer and choir director reflects his years of close contact with people throughout Europe and in the United States. NALR was the first publisher in the US to publish his music in English.

His songs, frequently using the rich poetic texts of Huub Oosterhuis, call for total involvement by the congregation, the choir, and musicians.

While Huijbers was a master musician, his burning concern was to empower the people to sing in celebration. The assembly is a "performing audience," and the music must bring to life what they celebrate.

Huijbers and Oosterhuis went on to release 11 collections of music, some with OCP Publications.

Paul Quinlan

Paul Quinlan's journey in the 1960s as one of the pioneer composers of the Folk Mass era, was chronicled in *Keep the Fire Burning*.[12] In the mid-70s, Quinlan moved on from the Jesuits and took up a staff position at NALR. He managed a short-lived satellite office in Los Angeles and eventually became one of the company's record producers.

Erich Sylvester

Born and raised in Cincinnati, Ohio, Erich Sylvester's musical journey began at a very young age in the Cathedral Boys Choir at Saint Peter in Chains Cathedral. They sang Gregorian chant, Palestrina and Mozart every Sunday in the pre-Vatican II days. But when he moved on to Saint Xavier High School, Sylvester took up the guitar, forming his own folk trio modeled after Peter, Paul & Mary. Through serendipity, he met that famous folk group's singer Peter Yarrow, who took Sylvester under his wing and invited him to perform commercial jingles that Yarrow had composed. Yarrow flew him and his group to New York, and they recorded the jingles at A&R Studio with Phil Ramone as engineer. From Yarrow and Ramone, Sylvester learned first-hand how to record on a professional level.

Sylvester eventually worked with John Denver and Mary Travers as a guitarist in their touring bands. In the early 70s, his friend Ed Gutfreund, a Cincinnati seminarian, inspired him to start composing liturgical music. Gutfreund was affiliated with NALR and that is how Sylvester ended up self-producing his first album with them, *The Best Is Yet to Come* that became one of NALR's 1972 bestsellers. Joe Wise described Sylvester's music as "…fresh, relaxed, exciting. The settings of the Mass texts are both singable and reverent to word." This collection includes the popular "Blessed Be God Forever," and "Stay with Me."[13]

Bruno was impressed with both the professional sound of Sylvester's album and the speed in which he produced it. Bruno invited him to join the NALR staff as executive producer, working with Carey Landry and Carol Jean Kinghorn on their *Hi God* albums, as well as the St. Louis Jesuits, and other NALR projects.

"Ray Bruno and Dan Onley gave us quite a bit of freedom," Sylvester recalled. "They would occasionally pop in at a recording studio and listen, but generally, I would just bring back rough mixes to the office and play it for them and give them updates on what we were doing."[14]

Sylvester also studied law on the side, received his law degree in 1975, and became NALR's legal advisor and copyright expert. He is now semi-retired in San Francisco and performs Hawaiian music internationally with his band, Hot Steel and Cool Ukelele.

Joe Zsigray

Born in 1953, Joe Zsigray hailed from Martins Ferry, Ohio, and made music "even when he was tiny," according to his mother. He attended high school at Divine Heart Seminary in Donaldson, Indiana and there learned the basics of reading and writing music as he taught himself to play multiple instruments.

After leaving the seminary, Zsigray recorded several albums with NALR, including *Berakah,* a collection of folk-style songs and hymns for the Eucharist and for the Liturgy of the Hours. His setting of "Psalm 104: Lord, Send Out Your Spirit" is still sung today, and is featured in OCP's *Glory & Praise, Third Edition* (2015). Zsigray worked with the developmentally disabled in Lorain County, and served as executive director of the Collingsworth Art Center in Toledo, Ohio. He passed away in 2014.

Ed Gutfreund

In the early 1960s, Ed Gutfreund went to Saint Xavier, a Jesuit-run high school in Cincinnati. He entered the seminary to study for the Archdiocese of Cincinnati, and became very involved in liturgical music as a composer and guitarist. He wrote a book that became an early manual on liturgical performance in the folk idiom: *With Lyre, Harp... and a Flatpick: The Folk Musician at Worship* (Cincinnati, OH: NALR, 1973). He was a folk music clinician at the very first convention of the National Association of Pastoral Musicians (NPM) in Scranton, Pennsylvania in 1978.

Gutfreund released several collections of liturgical music with NALR, including *From an Indirect Love* (1974), described by one critic as:

> A couple of acoustic rock songs with a rural edge and electric guitar ('Alleluia, Praise to The Lord' with nice dual leads, and 'Your People of Faith'). Sometimes a hint of early Talbot brothers. Pleasant cover of the Quaker hymn 'How Can I Keep from Singing?' along with a simple folk/gospel cover of 'Lights of the City.'[15]

Gutfreund was ordained a priest but he eventually moved on from ministry. At the time of this writing, he serves as a licensed professional counselor and massage therapist in Cincinnati, Ohio.

Sister Juliana Garza

Sister Juliana Garza is an illustrious member of the shortlist of female Catholic composers. Hailing from North Hollywood, California, she joined the community of the Sisters of Providence and settled in Seattle, Washington, after taking religious vows.

Sister is best remembered for her setting of the Lord's Prayer that is simply known as the "Echo Our Father," but her story is largely forgotten – until now.

Juliana was raised in an atmosphere conducive to the development of her talent. Her father, who taught Spanish classical guitar, interested his daughter at an early age in the instrument she now uses to accompany her songs. During her late teens Juliana began singing professionally, with folk and popular music her main interest.

At Providence Heights, during the period of study preparatory to her admission to vows, Sister Juliana began to write and compose her songs. 'The songs I write have already been written," says Sister Juliana. "They have been written in the wind, the sky, the trees, in all that pass me by. I have just paused to listen and write them down.'[16]

Sister Juliana worked in a variety of ministries, including serving the migrant farm workers in the Yakima Valley, and teaching in schools. Her first album, *Mixed Expressions,* was released on a private label and sold by her community. NALR heard about Sister through the many requests they received for her "Echo Our Father." A staffer finally met Sister in Spokane, Washington in 1973. Sister Juliana released *Communion Muse* on NALR, which included her popular Lord's Prayer setting.

Artists sometimes get into a formula rut where that formula either stays the same or deteriorates. But that's not the case here; after a six-year hiatus, some of which was back in her native California, Garza is back with a bang. The result is an avant-garde masterpiece that deserves to take its place with the best of them. "We Come to Your Table" is a masterpiece that made many a Communion special. [17]

Sister Juliana had a three-record contract with NALR but succeeding albums were never made. Her well-crafted music can be found on YouTube, and Boomer Catholics will never forget how her "Echo Our Father" was such a significant part of their prayer life in the 70s.

·■·

The NALR staff certainly kept their ear to the ground to stay on top of the latest industry trends. In November 1972, FEL Publications announced their groundbreaking "Annual Copy License" that allowed unlimited usage of any or all of the company's 1,250 copyrights for an annual fee of $100. Shortly afterward, NALR announced its own reprint policy.

The NALR Music Reprint License Program
It is now possible for any church, school or other group to print or copy music published by NALR in the forms most convenient to them, and to do so economically and legally! The actual application and associated paperwork is very simple – maybe 10 minutes per year!

What might take a little time is deciding which of the many options provided within the Program best fits your own situation.[18]

NALR's many situational licensing options were in response to FEL's blanket annual license. And for those parishes who didn't want to bother with printing out their own homemade folk hymnals, NALR offered one more creative innovation:

> If you have World Library's *Peoples Mass Book* in a recent edition, you have a darned nice basic book, attractive and with a good selection of music.

> But now we do offer a neat, practical, and very inexpensive way in which the many, many great and beautiful songs published by NALR can be ADDED to your Sunday or weekday celebrations without displacing any of the aids you are presently using.[19]

The *SING PRAISE!* books offered a large variety of popular NALR songs: "The Spirit Is a-Movin'" (Landry), "You Are the Way" (Wise), "Blessed Be God Forever" (Sylvester), "Sing, Hosanna, Sing" (Quinlan), "Only a Shadow" (Landry), "It's a Brand New Day" (Quinlan), "Go Now in Peace" (Wise), and more. These small inexpensive booklets would later feed NALR's phenomenally successful *Glory & Praise* contemporary songbooks.

Bruno's business experience as a retailer gave NALR an edge over other Catholic music publishers, many of whom had a former church musician at the helm. NALR was a member of the National Church Goods Association, a group of mega-Catholic catalog stores together with suppliers in religious articles, importers, vestments and vessels, candle manufacturers, and publishers. He sent Bob Lesinski, a pastoral musician with sales experience, on road trips to meet with retailers in their stores and write up some orders.

On one sales tour, Lesinski started in Chicago, and went through the large cities and small towns in Indiana, Ohio, lower Michigan, Pennsylvania, New Jersey, and New York—all within two weeks. At every stop, he played NALR's records and took large orders on the spot.[20]

"There was one store where the owner told me that NALR saved him from going out of business," Lesinski recalled:

> because so many dealers lost tons of money with obsolete inventories that resulted from the change in the liturgy. Dealers were caught with large quantities of Latin missals. But the new music was beginning to catch on in people's hearts. That, along with the 40 percent discount that Ray offered them, helped many dealers through a difficult transition in the Catholic market.[21]

At a time when most Catholic music publishers preferred to do business via direct mail order, NALR's personal relationships with the retailers paid off handsomely. At one point, more than 800 dealers were buying wholesale from Bruno's company.

By the end of 1973, Bruno and his staff could be justly proud of NALR's upward climb in the Catholic music industry. With the growing popularity of their music, submissions started pouring in from hundreds of would-be composers. It was Dan

Onley who started noticing requests for music by a group of young Jesuits in St. Louis. Intrigued, he obtained informal "purple ditto" copies of their songs, read through them, and brought them to Bruno's attention. These Jesuits would soon lead NALR and the Catholic Church in North America to soaring new heights.

---

[1] *Music in Catholic Worship,* Statement of the NCCB Committee on the Liturgy (Washington, DC., 1972; revised 1983).

[2] Canedo, Ken, *Keep the Fire Burning: The Folk Mass Revolution* (Portland, OR: Pastoral Press, 2009) 95-96.

[3] Interview with the author, June 19, 2017 in San Francisco, California.

[4] *Keeping Up,* Vol. III, No. 1 (Cincinnati, OH: NALR, Winter 1973), 16.

[5] Interview with the author, November 10, 2017, in Portland, Oregon.

[6] The later CD versions were re-recorded because the original masters had deteriorated.

[7] Interview with the author, November 15, 2004, by phone to Indianapolis, Indiana.

[8] *Keeping Up,* Vol. III, No. 1 (Cincinnati, OH: NALR, Winter 1973), 3.

[9] See Canedo, Ken, *Keep the Fire Burning: The Folk Mass Revolution* (Portland, OR: Pastoral Press, 2009) 85-87.

[10] Wise, Joe, *The Truth in Plenty: Entries from my journal, Vol. II / a rolling memoir* (Bloomington, IN: Balboa Press, 2017) 37.

[11] Jack Miffleton's story is told in Canedo, Ken, *Keep the Fire Burning: The Folk Mass Revolution* (Portland, OR: Pastoral Press, 2009) 96-98.

[12] Canedo, Ken, *Keep the Fire Burning: The Folk Mass Revolution* (Portland, OR: Pastoral Press, 2009) 80-82.

[13] *Keeping Up,* Vol. III, No. 1 (Cincinnati, OH: NALR, Winter 1973), 13.

[14] Interview with the author, June 19, 2017 in San Francisco, California.

[15] Review from *The Ancient Star-Song* blog: http://www.theancientstar-song.com/2009/06/ed-gutfreund/

[16] "Sister Juliana Records *Mixed Expressions,*" *The Providence Sister,* Vol. IV, No. 3 (Seattle, WA: Winter 1967), 11.

[17] Review from Positive Infinity website: https://www.vulcanhammer.org/2011/02/08/sister-juliana-garza-mixed-expressions-and-communion-muse/

[18] *Keeping Up,* 2.

[19] Ibid., 10.

[20] In secular music industry parlance, the person who personally meets dealers and places records in their stores is called a "rack jobber." Bruno's use of this technique again demonstrates his retail savvy.

[21] Interview with the author, October 19, 2009, from Grand Rapids, Michigan.

Hi God, Down Under

Hi God was an unqualified success when it was released in 1973. When Carey Landry and Carol Jean Kinghorn appeared at the Los Angeles Archdiocese's Religious Education Congress at the Anaheim Convention Center in 1975, NALR had the biggest sales day in its young history. "The reaction was wild," said Bob Lesinski, NALR Field Consultant.[1]

Landry and Kinghorn clearly tapped into a thirst for music composed specifically for children in a religious education setting. They became a complementary team. "Carol Jean did the teaching and I led the singing," recalled Landry. "That's what we knew and that's how we did our workshops."[2]

"I had also done a lot of gestures to the music," said Kinghorn, "because I know that when you use another sense, there is a greater understanding. Carey sang and I demonstrated the gestures that gave the children the freedom to feel, to move, and to be who they are."[3]

The workshop and concert requests poured in. Landry and Kinghorn were in such high demand that they brought their message to Melbourne, Australia, in 1979.

Kinghorn remembered, "The Archdiocese of Melbourne invited us to fly down and they had a wonderful plan for us. We did several different workshops every day over the course of three weeks."[4]

> Workshops focused on music: music in children's worship; music in religious education; music in worship for teenagers and young adults; evenings of prayerful music. Carol Jean led group participation in singing, gesturing and praying – integral parts of each workshop. Participants represented all groups within the community: children, teens, young adults, parents, priests, ministers, teachers, catechists. By all accounts, the tour got rave reviews.[5]

At Saint Mary's Parish in Mooroopna, Victoria, Fr. Maurice J. Duffy spoke of them at Mass: "In our village, we are known for various healthcare facilities, and we have a lot of elderly people who live in these facilities. But our church could not accommodate them because there was no way for them to come with their wheelchairs. Today, because of those two people," he gestured toward Carol Jean and Carey, "we can bring the people to the church and we can all be here together at Mass."

How did this happen? The priest shared the story. "We gathered all the children of the town into a big room and had them listen to *Hi God*. As they listened, they drew pictures of the images in their minds. They drew what those songs said to them, in their heart – whatever they felt and thought while listening to the music. Then we took the children's artwork and transformed them into stained glass windows."

The church had no access for people in wheelchairs. They moved the altar to the center of the church building and the priest faced one row of the new stained-glass windows.

They built wheelchair ramps on all four corners of the church so people with mobility challenges could join the liturgy and be part of the community.

Father beamed, "It's because of these two people from the other side of the world that all this came about." He smiled and gestured once again toward Carol Jean and Carey. "I want those two people to stand up."

"Oh, I tell you, I was in tears," said Carol Jean. "We were that little seed so far away, and our music inspired all this to happen." The children's stained-glass window designs would grace the cover of *Color the World with Song,* their 1982 collection of contemporary psalms for children.[6]

"I always look at it as the mustard seed parable," said Carey. *"Hi God* was a little, tiny seed that grew into a magnificent tree, far greater than we could ever imagine."[7]

---

[1] Interview with the author, October 19, 2009, via email from Grand Rapids, Michigan.
[2] Interview with the author, November 10, 2017 in Portland, Oregon.
[3] Ibid.
[4] Ibid.
[5] *Billboard,* September 27, 1980 (33).
[6] Carol Jean's father, Fred Kinghorn, designed a new image for the cover, based on photographs of Saint Mary's stained-glass windows.
[7] Interview with the author, November 10, 2017 in Portland, Oregon.

Chapter Five

"From Mountains High"
The St. Louis Jesuits, Early Years

Since the renewal of the Order of Mass following Vatican II, the ministry of the composer has been critical in creating a vernacular style of liturgical music that both engages the assembly and supports the Eucharistic ritual in keeping with the directives of the *Constitution on the Sacred Liturgy.*

Most Revered Donald W. Trautman, STD, SSL,
Bishop of Erie, Pennsylvania, Chairman of the
US Bishops' Committee on the Liturgy[1]

When you think of the notion of Providence in this whole deal, it is more than remarkable. It wasn't like we were trying to create a revolution.

Roc O'Connor, SJ[2]

Everyone wants to live on top of the mountain, but all the happiness and growth occurs while you're climbing it.

Andy Rooney[3]

When the Vatican's Congregation for Divine Worship promulgated the new Rite of Christian Initiation of Adults (RCIA) on the Solemnity of the Epiphany, January 6, 1972, liturgists and catechists were ecstatic. Baptism for adults was now restored to a catechetical journey of several stages that had its roots in the Church of the fourth century. Most notably, the whole parish community was now invited to become involved in a journey of support for inquirers who felt called by the Holy Spirit to become fully initiated members of the Roman Catholic Church. The journey culminated in the celebration of the Sacraments of Initiation – Baptism, Confirmation, and Eucharist – during the Easter Vigil in the Holy Night.

For Jesuit students, the liturgies of Holy Week were the high point of the year. The Sacred Triduum required meticulous planning. But the Easter Vigil, so closely tied with the RCIA, was very sweet indeed, with the Blessing of the Easter Fire, the procession of the Paschal Candle in a darkened church, the solemn chanted proclamation of the *Exsultet,* the high drama of salvation history in the nine readings from the Old and New Testaments, the intonation of the Easter Alleluia, and the celebration of the Sacraments of Initiation after the homily. All this in one dynamic liturgy!

The Jesuits at Saint Louis University (SLU) had a strong commitment to the renewal liturgy. They had regular liturgy planning meetings, and took seriously the Council's call for the "full, conscious and active participation" of the assembly. On Sunday mornings, two chapels were filled to capacity, as the Jesuits welcomed women from nearby religious communities, SLU theology students from around the world, and Catholics and seekers from around the St. Louis region.

"They'd be spilling into the side chapels along the back and up into the choir loft," remembered Dan Schutte. "My last two years there we had to give out tickets for the Easter Triduum, because the fire department was upset and had put limits on how many people we could have in there."[4]

Word had spread about the lively liturgies that involved the full participation of the people in all the ministries of the Mass: reader, acolyte, hospitality, extraordinary ministers of the Eucharist, and most especially, music ministry. In 1971, Schutte got together with a small group of Jesuit classmates at Fusz Memorial Chapel to plan music for the Easter morning Mass.

"We planned the Triduum some weeks before, but had left Easter Sunday till the last minute," Schutte recalled.

> Someone in the group said, 'Dan, why don't you write an Easter hymn, something new and joyful, something that would express the energy of Easter Sunday morning.' 'And what might the text be?' I asked. After a brief discussion the group agreed that Psalm 98, an Easter season psalm, would be a good starting place. For myself, I already knew that I wanted to craft a piece that made people feel like they wanted to dance, and so began with that as a goal. It was one of the few songs in my lifetime that was completed in just a couple days.[5]

The song Dan composed brought smiles to his friends, and inspired the diverse assembly in Fusz to immediately sing and sway to its joyful 3/4-time guitar strum.

> Sing a new song unto the Lord.
> Let your song be sung from mountains high.
> Sing a new song unto the Lord,
> singing Alleluia.

John Foley, Bob Dufford, Robert "Roc" O'Connor, Tim Manion, and Dan Schutte were at various stages of their Jesuit formation when they came together at Saint Louis University in the early 1970s. Foley has always been grateful for that serendipity. "I believe grace was the glue that held us together for so many years."[6]

John Foley, son of Paul and Marjorie Foley, was born in Peoria, Illinois in 1939. Shortly after his birth, the family relocated to Wichita, Kansas, where his father opened a Caterpillar tractor dealership. As a young boy, John showed an early aptitude for music.

> I was a composer from the time I was a little kid. I started piano lessons at about five and, by the time I got out of high school, I was a good classical

pianist. I thought about joining the Jesuits when I was a senior in high school in Wichita, but I was more interested in romance, and I was still interested in music. I put it aside, and I went to Regis College in Denver. When I started taking philosophy in college, I really wanted to be a philosopher. I was drawn by too many things.[7]

At Regis College, Foley took a special interest in the structure and composition of classical music. He had to scale a wall at night to sneak into a room with a piano to try his hand at composing sonatas. John made plans to pursue music, and a seed had been planted.

> I went to music school at Wichita State the year after I graduated from college, and the Jesuits still seemed pretty good. I did not know anything about the Jesuit novitiate or anything like that; I didn't know anything about discernment. I just sort of asked God, 'Which one do you want me to do?' I made God take responsibility for it.[8]

John wistfully remembered how he took up guitar out of musical necessity:

> There was a surprise waiting at the Jesuit novitiate when I entered at age 22: there was no accessible piano. Just for fun, I asked a fellow novice to show me some guitar chords. I had already written choral music for choir, organ and individual instruments, but suddenly the guitar-group trend began in the church. Since I was a classical musician, I had never dreamed of writing popular church music. The guitar sort of fell into my hands.[9]

Robert J. Dufford (nicknamed "Duff" by his friends) was born in Chicago in 1943 and grew up in Omaha, Nebraska. His father Jack sang and played harmonica and piano with the Four Kernie's quartet.

> When I started going to Mass around sixth grade, I was singing in choirs and learned all the chants. That continued into high school. I'd mow the lawn and sing at the top of my voice, making up songs or singing songs I knew. A lot of it was connected with the liturgy.[10]

Dufford would not learn to play the guitar until he entered the Jesuit novitiate, inspired by a fellow novice named John Foley, who had just picked up the guitar himself. Foley shared with Dufford some songs that he had composed. Clearly impressed, Dufford decided to learn guitar and begin writing songs himself.

> I was sitting in my room, working on this little chord pattern, and I was singing a melody against it. This was in St. Louis, about nine months after I had gotten a guitar. I had just learned to play a couple of months before that. I had just started to notate this little song when a guy from New York Province came in and said, 'What are you doing?' He asked me to sing the song, so I did. Then he said, 'We gotta use that for Good Friday.' I said, 'What?' I had no idea it was going to touch other people.[11]

Roc O'Connor's nickname comes from the capital letters in his first and last names: Robert O'Connor. He was born in 1949 in Southern California.

> My father, Robert F. O'Connor, Sr., was from Georgia, and my mother, Mary Elizabeth Cotter hailed from Omaha, Nebraska. After the war, dad reenlisted and was sent near Los Angeles. Mom moved out there to live with her first cousins and work as a nurse. They met at Saint James Parish in Redondo Beach, California, during a CYO event.[12]

The family moved back to Omaha. Roc is the oldest of eight children, including one brother, Mike, and six sisters: Joanne, Theresa, Patty, Cathy, Colleen, and Karen. They attended Saint Pius X School in Omaha. By great coincidence, when Roc made his First Communion in second grade, Bob Dufford was in eighth grade as a member of the school's first graduating class.

> I went to Creighton Prep, the Jesuit High School in Omaha. There were some great men who taught me. Since I worked two years at the school and Jesuit Community switchboard, I got to know them. On retreat, while attempting to draw a picture of the chapel, I had a powerful experience of God saying, basically, 'This is where you belong.' I wept having never felt such love and presence. Upon returning home, I promptly forgot about it because I wanted to date this girl I had just met. But she was dating another guy. Rats. Around April, I remembered that experience. I applied around prom time and was accepted four to five weeks later after graduation.[13]

Unlike the other members of the St. Louis Jesuits, Roc did not come from a musical family.

> What I wanted to do was be a drummer and play rock-and-roll. My parents, rather wisely, got my brother and me an electric guitar, and we took lessons. I basically learned one song, 'Gloria' by the Shadows of Knight. I learned a ton when I entered the novitiate. There were two guys a year ahead of me who showed me a lot about chords and finger-picking. We had a novice rock-and-roll band called Mogen David and the Grapes of Wrath. I finally got to play drums! It was great fun. Schutte was a year ahead of me. I was learning to play while he composed his early songs: 'You Are Near,' 'Yahweh, the Faithful One,' and others.[14]

Born in 1947 at Neenah, Wisconsin, Dan Schutte was a self-professed "band geek," playing clarinet and saxophone as a grade school student at Saint Mary's Visitation School in Elm Grove, Wisconsin, before picking up guitar as a junior at Marquette University High School. At Marquette, the students attended daily Mass, with music directed by Jesuit "scholastics"—young Jesuits who taught in schools during their "regency" years between the philosophy and theology schools.

"We mostly sang traditional English hymns at Latin Mass. One of the Jesuits taught us Gelineau's setting of Psalm 23. I fell in love with Gelineau's psalmody because it had that connection to chant, and yet it sounded so modern."[15] Dan had plans to become a pediatrician until some Jesuits steered him in another direction.

"I entered the Jesuit novitiate after high school with that music background. It was at the time guitars were being introduced into the Mass. Along with others, I began to introduce guitar-accompanied music into the liturgy."[16] The *Hymnal for Young Christians* was in vogue, and that meant the music of Ray Repp and such Folk Mass standards as "They'll Know We Are Christians" and "Sons of God."

> I'd never written music before in my life, except to make up little melodies as I'd sit at my grandfather's piano. We had this gentle Jesuit, Father Barney Portz, on the faculty. He was a big influence on Roc, Duff and me. He was the choir director, and he recognized musical gifts in us. He'd look at some songs I had composed and he'd offer us his comments and suggestions. At some point he'd say, 'You know, I think it's ready for us to try at Mass; let's see what happens.' He was really the one who first saw the possibility of my music and encouraged me.[17]

Tim Manion was born in 1951 in St. Louis, a Catholic town centered around parish life, school life and sports.

> I loved music when I was a kid, but other than the normal kid things, the first thing I really perceived was a solid desire to be a Jesuit. In high school, we had this very cool Mass at midnight on Saturday. People went on dates and then came to midnight Mass. I got involved in this little music group that played for that. There wasn't anybody to play bass, and one guy thought he could teach me to play four notes. When we needed a guitar player, I swapped to that. That was my first exposure to that kind of thing. I did it long enough that it carried over to the novitiate.[18]

For Jesuits in the Midwest, students from various regional novitiates were brought together at Saint Louis University to study philosophy and theology.

Dan Schutte recalled, "People who were in charge of Jesuit formation decided it would be a good thing for the guys to have a wider experience of the Society of Jesus in the United States. So, we were all of a sudden thrown together with all these other Jesuits."[19]

These were the days when Jesuit students studied together, dined together, prayed together, and relaxed together. Recreation did not mean going out for a good time on the town. Rather, it meant athletic activity or music. In the 60s and 70s, the five who became the St. Louis Jesuits sang at daily Mass. Foley received formal education in classical music, but the men were also influenced by popular music of their times. The guitar became as essential as a cassock for many Jesuits, who spent many evenings together singing the songs of the day. The guitar became useful in the classrooms where they taught CCD (religious education) to children. And, as the Folk Mass grew in popularity, it became an important accompaniment to the liturgy.

Dufford and Foley had finished philosophy, but they, too, were stationed in St. Louis, studying theology in preparation for ordination. Both had continued to compose music, but things had changed. Foley had grown tired of being the point man for Jesuit liturgy: "I was the only one doing it. I had to play all the Masses, and it was too much."

After years of work in the field, he had largely given up on the [liturgical] genre and was now producing a folk album, *Ways to Get Through,* with a fellow Jesuit theology student, John Kavanaugh. For his part, Dufford saw himself headed toward an advanced degree in mathematics. Music was consequently diminishing in importance.[20]

Despite this, both Foley and Dufford were intrigued enough to occasionally join Schutte, O'Connor, and Manion. They pooled together their existing songs as the readings suggested, and composed new songs for those occasions that were lacking in musical support.

> These inspired liturgies grew to be widely known throughout the St. Louis area. Many found that the music of these men helped them pray in a way they had not experienced before. The pieces were easy to learn, but one did not tire of singing them. The lyrics, drawn from Scripture, allowed people to sing wholeheartedly because the words expressed the prayer of every human heart.[21]

The composers soon saw an unforeseen demand for their music. Schutte explained. "Whenever we introduced a new song, people would come up to us after Mass and asked, 'May we have a copy of that?'"[22] With no thought to compensation, the Jesuit composers gave away their music via the medium utilized by educational institutions everywhere: purple ditto, all hand stenciled by Schutte himself.[23] Thus, in their own primitive way, the songs went viral.

"'For You Are My God' is the third piece I wrote in the 'SLJ' style," John Foley recalled. "I was composing only for local liturgy, so the biggest surprise of all was when I learned that the Charismatic movement had made a theme song of it for their huge gathering in Notre Dame stadium!"[24]

> Saint Louis University was home to the Institute for Religious Formation (IRF), an international training center for spiritual directors. And for their daily and weekend liturgies, these students went to Fusz Memorial, providing the young Jesuits with an open-minded, enthusiastic forum in which to try new things. They were also an unforeseen market. When IRF students completed their programs, they took home with them not only diplomas, but also sheaves of dittos.[25] Because of this ditto sharing, their music was being sung in Guam, the Philippines, Australia, China, Africa, and all over the United States.

The ditto copies made their way to Cincinnati, and into the hands of Ray Bruno and Dan Onley, who were working hard to get North American Liturgy Resources off the ground. Onley started discussing with Bruno about the possibility of publishing these Jesuit composers from St. Louis.

Meanwhile, back at Fusz, it was dawning on the composers that they would soon be leaving SLU. Schutte recalled:

> I remember sitting in my room with Bob. It was on our brains that at the end of the following year, Bob and John would be ordained and go off someplace

to be assigned. I was going off to regency and so was Roc. There was going to be a huge exodus of the core people who led the liturgies and the music there.

So, Bob and I brainstormed. Why don't we get copies of all our music and bind it all together in a book? We would print the copies, punch holes, and put them in a loose-leaf binder. That soon morphed to, 'Well, if we're going to do this, why don't we do it a little bit nicer?' So, I would hand-stencil the notated music. People loved John's earlier music, and now he had a new song, 'I Will Sing.' Let's ask John if he wants to have his music thrown into this little book we're planning to make? Tim also has a song. We can put them all together so that after we leave, we would have a whole book to give to them.

And then we thought, 'Who's going to take care of distributing it? Where are the copies going to be?' So, Duff asked the Jesuit Mission Bureau of the Missouri Province if they would do it. They said, 'Of course. This is part of our ministry.'

Dan and Bob discussed the idea with John Foley, Tim Manion, and John Kavanagh, who all agreed it would be a wonderful resource.[26]

During his free time, Dan Schutte began hand-scripting the pieces for a songbook. These were the days before computer notation programs. There were also no funds available to have the score professionally engraved. All total, there were 107 pages of music and chord charts. That same year, the others began the process of recording the songs.[27]

"We came to the point where we needed some money to go into this little home studio and do these recordings," Schutte recalled.

We were going to need money to manufacture these cassette tapes to distribute to people, and to print the book. My dear mom and dad came along and wrote us a check and gave it to our Jesuit superiors and said, 'We want to support this.' So our superiors appointed Bob as our treasurer. That's how we paid for expenses before NALR came on the scene.[28] The basement studio had air-conditioning but when you turned it on there was a low-grade hum that was awful—and went right onto the tape. So, we had to turn the air conditioner off during the recording and do these songs over and over. And then, of course, when people got hot and tired, the pitch started going off. Those basement tapes were done on a two-track recorder, two-track stereo. It was all recorded live, so you can imagine having to get voices and instruments and everything balanced so everything could happen all at once.[29]

Roc O'Connor recalled:

I remember playing guitar at the sessions John Foley led in the basement. I had originally learned to play John's songs from other musicians. So, when John showed us how he wanted the tempo and strum to go, I was flabbergasted! It was so different from what I had been playing. Yet it made complete sense.

We all figured that this collection would be a 'terminal project.' Since people connected with St. Louis for this music, it was arranged that our music would be sold out of Fusz Memorial. Dan and John had each submitted their songs to publishers in the year or so before Spring 1973. Each were turned down.[30]

John Foley remembered:

Dan Onley came to see me and said, 'We're very hungry, and we've heard about your music.' When I told him we were planning to self-publish, he offered NALR to be our publisher. We were very uncertain at first; maybe it was excessive naiveté, but we just wanted to have something to give out. I had been interested in publishing, but after having [received] so many rejection letters, thought maybe it wasn't meant to be.[31]

"The tracks come from three different sources," said Dan. "One was from the basement studio at Fusz Memorial. The dominant number of tracks came from three days that we spent in the home studio of Kent Kesterson in West County outside of St. Louis. And there were a few tracks that we recorded live from our community liturgies.

We had a little more control with Kent's four-track. Again, the recording was all done live. There were no overdubs. We were used to doing live liturgies. Those three days in the home studio were right at the end of the school year, so we finished exams and had a core group of friends and a few Jesuits who were willing to stay around a few days before taking off.[32]

"Coming up with a title for the project was big," said Roc.

We went through the entire Bible looking for phrases that might somehow describe our intentions for putting this collection together. Duff came up with some fun ones: *A Plague of Frogs; What to Sing Until the Messiah Comes; And They Did It a Third Time.* I don't recall who actually who found the title *Neither Silver Nor Gold* (from Acts 3:1-10) but I liked it immediately.[33]

The Jesuits faced the challenge of finding a piece of art for the cover of their first songbook and record. They approached Donald-David Fehrenbach, a fellow Jesuit and artist who lived with Dan and Roc at Fusz Memorial, who could not have been more gracious in accepting the task.[34] "Donald ended up contributing covers to all our collections except one—*The Steadfast Love*." Roc recalled. "He was a very gifted artist and died too young."[35]

There was one more important item to put in place. As NALR stepped up production on the new album, Ray Bruno kept asking the composers, "Guys! We need a name! We need some way of identifying you."

After some discussion, they decided to keep things simple:

Neither Silver Nor Gold: Liturgical music from St. Louis Jesuits.

"Not THE St. Louis Jesuits," Schutte explained modestly. "We were just Jesuits from St. Louis."[36] But to all those university students and alumni and locals who experienced this music first-hand, the name was logical and catchy. It instantly identified the young composers who elevated the liturgies at Fusz Memorial with their Scripture-based lyrics and soaring melodies. The public at large would soon join the Saint Louis University community in recognizing that it was THE St. Louis Jesuits who invited people to let their song be sung from mountains high.[37]

> The Jesuit composers never gave much thought to what would happen next. Dan and Roc left to teach on the Lakota Sioux reservation in South Dakota, while Bob Dufford went to teach at Creighton Preparatory School in Omaha. John Foley stayed in St. Louis as a member of the Jesuit formation team at Fusz Memorial. Tim had already left the Jesuit community by then, and was living and going to school in St. Louis.[38] When the philosophy student Mass at Fusz Memorial moved to Saint Francis Xavier College Church, Tim became choir director for that Sunday liturgy.[39]

Then, something extraordinary happened. Sales of *Neither Silver Nor Gold* went through the roof!

> Their song book and record album, *Neither Silver Nor Gold,* is, in my opinion, the most consistently high-level collection of liturgical songs now in use. The lyrics tend to be either directly scriptural or very closely tied to Scripture, and are almost, without exception, not only poetic but intelligible. The music has the possibility of permanence that only comes about through the right mixture of sophistication and immediate attractiveness.
>
> -James L. Empereur, SJ for *Celebration* magazine, 1974[40]

> The collection of music entitled *Neither Silver Nor Gold* by the St. Louis Jesuits was the first extensive resource available to folk musicians which employed direct and close scriptural text sources with accessible melodies and simple guitar harmonization. It marked a clear change from music that seemed to focus first upon the assembly and its actions; rather, the Jesuits' music assumed the assembly's understanding of its own role, and attempted by the use of scriptural texts (especially psalms) to directly express the assembly's prayer through music. In this regard, it moved the direction of "folk" repertoire back toward the mainstream of Catholic liturgical expression, and paved the way for liturgical "folk" music to be viewed as textually compatible with more traditional and formal musical forms.
>
> -Marty Haugen, *Pastoral Music*[41]

What you have and what you sent me is indeed of very great value, especially as a testimony of Christian faith, presented in beautiful lyrical compositions, and it is no wonder that earlier antagonisms and prejudice have melted away. I would hope that through your music and song, which are such powerful means of communication, many will walk more steadily. Not through gifts of gold and silver, but through what you have to give.

-Letter dated October 11, 1974, to John Foley from Pedro Arrupe, SJ, Superior General of the Society of Jesus, Rome[42]

Clearly, their music struck a chord with liturgical America and beyond. John Foley thought it was time to get the guys back together.

"We need to look at what's been happening this year with our music," John suggested to his friends, "to look at what it's doing in the life of communities at prayer, and in the life of the American Church. Maybe we need to ask ourselves whether or not God has something bigger in mind."[43]

After years of finding their voices as composers and singers; after fine-tuning their newly crafted songs; after months of basement recording sessions and painstaking hand-stenciled notation work; and after moving on to new assignments and separate adventures – what could possibly be bigger than the mountain they just climbed?

Another mountain beckoned these Jesuits from St. Louis—a mountain carved from earthen vessels.

[1] Gale, Mike, editor, *The St. Louis Jesuits: Thirty Years* (Portland, OR, Oregon Catholic Press, 2006), 15.
[2] McDermott, SJ, Jim, "Sing a New Song," *America: The National Catholic Review.* May 23, 2005.
[3] Quote attributed to Andy Rooney from his "Enlightened Perspectives."
[4] McDermott, SJ, Jim, "Sing a New Song," *America: The National Catholic Review.* May 23, 2005.
[5] Interview with the author, August 30, 2014 in San Francisco, California.
[6] Gale, Mike, editor, *The St. Louis Jesuits: Thirty Years* (Portland, OR, Oregon Catholic Press, 2006) 105.
[7] Ibid, 100.
[8] Ibid, 100.
[9] Ibid, 105.
[10] Ibid, 90.
[11] Ibid, 91.
[12] Interview with the author, October 23, 2017, via email from Milwaukee, Wisconsin.
[13] Ibid.
[14] Gale, Mike, editor, *The St. Louis Jesuits: Thirty Years* (Portland, OR, Oregon Catholic Press, 2006) 120, plus interview with the author, October 16, 2017.
[15] Interview with the author, August 30, 2014 in San Francisco.
[16] Gale, Mike, editor, *The St. Louis Jesuits: Thirty Years* (Portland, OR, Oregon Catholic Press, 2006), 130.
[17] Ibid, 130.
[18] Ibid, 110.
[19] Interview with the author, August 30, 2014 in San Francisco.
[20] McDermott, SJ, Jim, "Sing a New Song," *America: The National Catholic Review.* May 23, 2005.
[21] Gale, Mike, editor, *The St. Louis Jesuits: Thirty Years* (Portland, OR, Oregon Catholic Press, 2006) 21.
[22] Interview with the author, August 30, 2014 in San Francisco.
[23] In the days before laser printers and photocopiers, schools and churches printed multiple copies of bulletins, class notes and songbooks via a primitive medium called ditto. The writer simply typed or handwrote text on a two-ply master sheet. The second sheet was coated with a layer of colored wax, and the pressure of typing or writing on the top sheet transferred the colored wax to its backside, creating a stencil for printing. The completed top sheet was attached to a drum on a "spirit duplicator" or ditto machine through which paper was fed by a hand crank. A sweet-smelling alcohol caused the stencil to print out in the color purple. Many school children of this era remember bringing freshly dittoed copies to their noses as teachers distributed them in their classroom. Mimeograph was an alternate reproduction technique that utilized black ink. These inexpensive printing systems were a big factor in the speedy distribution of the liturgical music of the 1960s and 70s.
[24] Interview with the author, April 2009, for CD release of *Neither Silver Nor Gold.*
[25] McDermott, SJ, Jim, "Sing a New Song," *America: The National Catholic Review.* May 23, 2005.
[26] Interview with the author, August 30, 2014 in San Francisco.

[27] Gale, Mike, editor, *The St. Louis Jesuits: Thirty Years* (Portland, OR, Oregon Catholic Press, 2006) 29.

[28] Interview with the author, August 30, 2014 in San Francisco.

[29] Interview with the author, April 2009, for CD release of *Neither Silver Nor Gold*.

[30] Ibid.

[31] Gale, Mike, editor, *The St. Louis Jesuits: Thirty Years* (Portland, OR, Oregon Catholic Press, 2006) 100.

[32] Interview with the author, April 2009, for CD release of *Neither Silver Nor Gold*.

[33] Ibid.

[34] Gale, Mike, editor, *The St. Louis Jesuits: Thirty Years* (Portland, OR, Oregon Catholic Press, 2006) 38.

[35] Interview with the author, April 2009, for CD release of *Neither Silver Nor Gold*.

[36] Interview with the author, August 30, 2014 in San Francisco.

[37] John Kavanagh was a fellow Jesuit student who contributed songs to *Neither Silver Nor Gold*. John Foley paid tribute to him in the 2009 CD release of their first album. "The tenor voice of John Kavanagh, S.J., is an integral part of the NSNG recording, and his haunting compositions are still used today to great effect. This is a testimony to John's talent, since the four liturgical songs on this album are the only ones he has published: "A Banquet Is Prepared," "To You I Lift Up My Soul," "God Is Love," and "All Things Have Their Time." John Kavanagh left liturgical music after NSNG in order to work on his doctorate in philosophy. He became a very popular teacher of medical ethics at Saint Louis University." (from liner notes for the CD release of *Neither Silver Nor Gold*.)

[38] Gale, Mike, editor, *The St. Louis Jesuits: Thirty Years* (Portland, OR, Oregon Catholic Press, 2006), 32.

[39] Per John Foley, S.J., interview with the author, October 13, 2017 via email from St. Louis, Missouri.

[40] Gale, Mike, editor, *The St. Louis Jesuits: Thirty Years* (Portland, OR, Oregon Catholic Press, 2006), 37.

[41] Haugen, Marty, *Pastoral Music* (April-May 1984), 16-17.

[42] Gale, Mike, editor, *The St. Louis Jesuits: Thirty Years* (Portland, OR, Oregon Catholic Press, 2006), 36.

[43] Interview with the author, March 2015, for CD release of *Earthen Vessels: 40th Anniversary Edition*.

Chapter Six

"The Steadfast Love"
The St. Louis Jesuits, Later Years

All that a man knows, and needs to know, is found in Berkeley.
-A Vision by W.B. Yeats[1]

As my former students, they have gone beyond their teacher.
-James Empereur, SJ[2]

The composers of *Neither Silver Nor Gold* didn't think of themselves as a band or a singing group. No concerts. No radio play. No personal appearances. Their album contained four LP records and sold for $18.00, a princely sum in those days. By music industry marketing standards, *Neither Silver Nor Gold* should have flopped. And yet, it became the bestselling Catholic liturgical album of 1974. How did that happen?

First, there were 57 songs, including a Mass setting. In an era when Catholic musicians were hungry for new music, this large volume alone was enticing. But all the songs in the world wouldn't count for anything unless they were *good* songs with exquisitely crafted melodies. And these songs were psalm settings and Old Testament canticles, songs based on the Gospels and the New Testament letters, upbeat songs for gathering and sending, reflective songs, and songs for the liturgical seasons. *Neither Silver Nor Gold* was the cumulative work of several years of composing for liturgies based on the three-year cycle of readings, and that was another factor.

Another appealing element of this collection was the way John, Bob, Dan, Roc, and Tim played their guitars. The sound of a typical parish folk ensemble was a source of derision for critics of the genre.

> It wasn't just the fact of guitars at liturgy that shocked many people; it was also the way those guitars were played. Even on the earliest Folk Mass records, producers took care to create a compelling sound that utilized the full versatility of the instrument: finger-picking, colorful lead lines, and a variety of different strums, emulating the folk music sound heard on secular records. Such subtlety was lost on many parish guitarists, who enthusiastically played the same basic 4/4 strum on every song.[3]

The St. Louis Jesuits included fingerpicking charts and strum patterns in their songbooks, along with the chords. And they taught a whole generation of guitarists how to play Open-D tuning, in which the lower E string is dropped down to D, requiring a different way of making chords that gave a more compelling and resonant sound. Dan Schutte reflected on that:

> It was one of those integral things that grew out of our experience of doing music for liturgy. In our developing sense of liturgy and prayer, we probably felt an innate need for a guitar accompaniment that was more than the strum-dee-dum thing. We wanted the guitar to express the prayer of some of those scriptural texts in a way that pure strumming would not accomplish.[4]

And there was one more element of appeal in their music: the simple but effective vocal harmonies. The Jesuits arranged their music for the community *choir,* not just for themselves as solo singers. This was an accessible contemporary choral model that parish choirs could follow, instead of trying to imitate the sound of Peter, Paul & Mary or The Kingston Trio.

Is it any wonder that the music of *Neither Silver Nor Gold* burst into instant popularity, despite no touring or concert appearances by the composers? This new music by the Jesuits of St. Louis was filling an obvious gap in the so-called "folk" repertoire for liturgy.

Earthen Vessels

The success of *Neither Silver Nor Gold* took the composers by surprise. With the blessing and support of their superiors, the five regrouped in Berkeley, California, during the summer of 1974 at Shalom House, the student residence of the Jesuit School of Theology. Tim had moved on from the Jesuits, but he wanted to come, and the others welcomed him with open arms. For the next five weeks, they would live together, pray together, and compose music. They did not have the goal of creating a new album. Their summer together was to be an extended retreat, a time to discern where the Holy Spirit was leading them. *Neither Silver Nor Gold* was a grace-filled confirmation that the gift of music was a seed that God had planted in them. Perhaps it was something they needed to pay attention to in a greater way.

"It was a central moment," remembered Manion. "It was the first time that we acknowledged to ourselves and to each other that we were trying to do something together that was more than a bunch of guys hanging out and working on this Mass ritual program."[5]

In Berkeley, each composer worked on individual songs, then shared them with the group for feedback, constructive criticism, and encouragement. John Foley had the most formal music training, and he mentored the others in the technical aspects of composing. As always, they turned to sacred Scripture as a source for their lyrics.[6]

They bonded as seekers, as musicians, as brothers; and the Spirit blessed them with the inspiration to compose songs that would become an iconic part of the modern liturgical repertoire.

"Duff struggled so long and hard with 'Be Not Afraid,'" Schutte recalled. "He had played the melody in the first phrase years before. Everybody said, 'Duff, you have to work at finishing it.' That summer in Berkeley, he finally did."[7] Dufford also composed "Sing to the Mountains," an eventual parish favorite, and "My Son Has Gone Away," a moving reflection on the parable of the Prodigal Son from the father's viewpoint.

Berkeley gave Roc O'Connor an opportunity to develop as a composer. Although he had contributed his fine guitar work to *Neither Silver Nor Gold,* that collection did not contain any songs composed by him. That summer, he penned "Trust in the Lord" that appeared on *A Dwelling Place* (their third album), and the stirring "Seek the Lord" that appeared on *Earthen Vessels.* The latter is based on Isaiah 55 and has become a staple in the parish repertoire, especially during Lent.

> Seek the Lord whose mercy abounds;
> call aloud to God who is near.
>
> Today is the day and now the proper hour
> to forsake our sinful lives and turn to the Lord.

Tim Manion composed the popular "This Alone" based on Psalm 25. It would appear on *Lord of Light* in 1981.

> One thing I ask, this alone I seek,
> to dwell in the house of the Lord all my days.
> For one day within your temple
> heals every day alone.
> O Lord, bring me to your dwelling.

That summer, Dan Schutte composed three songs: "What You Hear in the Dark," "If the Lord Does Not Build," and the upbeat "Though the Mountains May Fall," which became the opening track on *Earthen Vessels.*

John Foley was inspired during the summer retreat to return to composing in earnest. His Berkeley compositions included "If God Is for Us," "Turn to Me," "Praise the Lord, My Soul," "Take, Lord, Receive," and "Earthen Vessels," the gentle song that became the title track of their new album.

> We hold a treasure, not made of gold,
> in earthen vessels wealth untold;
> one treasure only: the Lord, the Christ,
> in earthen vessels.

It's interesting to note that these composers generally did not write songs together. Most of the songs on the St. Louis Jesuit albums are solo efforts, but they did collaborate. That summer in Berkeley they were learning how to work together. Dufford remembered it this way. "Out in Berkeley, we were working on just being a group together and learning how to do music together because we thought maybe we should continue this somehow. We didn't know where it was going to go from there."[8]

When their publisher Ray Bruno heard the group had created such a large number of new songs, he invited them to produce a second collection and flew them out to Cincinnati to record at Counterpart Creative Studios. Bruno pulled out the stops with a 15-voice choir, woodwinds, timpani, and a string section arranged by John Pell. The resulting album, *Earthen Vessels,* was released in 1975 and would see eventual sales of more than one million units across several formats: LP record, cassette, CD, and digital playlist.

First Concert Appearances

With two successful albums under their belt, NALR felt it was time for the St. Louis Jesuits to finally hit the road. They approached the idea with caution. Their hesitancy arose from a realization that the music they wrote was intended for people to pray with, most often in a liturgical setting.

"We had no intention of 'performing' these songs on a stage," said Manion. "These are liturgical songs, meant to be sung by the people at Mass."[9]

"NALR used to sponsor a summer Festival of Song and Celebration," Schutte recalled:

> and we were invited to the 1975 event in Cincinnati, along with Joe Wise, Carey Landry, Ed Gutfreund, and Erich Sylvester. We went to this convention hall, walked in, and there was the NALR booth and all these big posters of composers up on the wall. And we thought, 'Oh, my gosh. What are we getting into?' And we went up on stage and did a few songs. We had no idea what the heck we were doing, really. We knew how to play for Mass and were pretty confident about that, but this was a whole different thing. I remember us talking to ourselves about trying to be true to the music and to the ministerial part of this thing that got bigger than us.[10]

By all accounts, the St. Louis Jesuits were an inspiring performance group, despite their initial reluctance.

A Dwelling Place

In the year that followed, John, Bob, Roc, Dan, and Tim did not identify themselves as the "St. Louis Jesuits." They were each involved in their own ministerial assignments or in academic pursuits. But they continued to write songs that served the worship life of their communities at College Church in St. Louis, Missouri, Holy Rosary, and Saint Francis Missions in South Dakota, or Saint John Church in Omaha, Nebraska. New songs were used almost immediately at liturgy, giving each composer an opportunity to receive appreciated feedback that helped shape their compositions into final form. Their Jesuit superiors approved and encouraged their music ministry.

NALR was pleased with the sales of their albums and invited the five composers to come once again to Cincinnati to record a new collection. They brought many songs to the studio and settled on 14 for their new album. Many of these titles are still familiar to congregations today because of continued placement in hymnals and missals. The album took its title, *A Dwelling Place,* from John Foley's song, based on Ephesians 3.

> I fall on my knees to the Father of Jesus,
> the Lord who has shown us the glory of God.
>
> May Christ find a dwelling place of faith in our hearts.
> May our lives be rooted in love.
>
> ©1976, John B. Foley, S.J., and OCP. All rights reserved.

The overall sound of this new collection continued the choral folk sound of *Earthen Vessels* that had quickly become the trademark of the St. Louis Jesuits. "We started recording *A Dwelling Place* at the studio in Cincinnati," remembered NALR producer Erich Sylvester, "and, unfortunately, there was a technical issue with the recording board. We noticed it; we could hear it."

Bob Dufford continues the story. "We listened to the tracks and there were little distortions here or there. A song would top out, which meant that someone wasn't watching out for the peak moments. All the guys heard it.

"We figured out it was a problem with the DBX noise reduction system that was in vogue at the time. We started calling around to other studios and kept getting the same response: 'You'll need to go to Nashville for that kind of system.'" "But Roc and Tim kept calling around," said Dufford:

> and they finally found a studio in Cincinnati that had the same system. So, we took the tapes over there. The choir tracks were fine. So were the string tracks, thank God, because it would have been expensive to bring them back in to rerecord. It was the guitar tracks that were problematic.
>
> We planned for 14 tracks on the album and had only recorded half of them. So, we set to work on recording the remaining tracks. Foley had gone back to St. Louis for a short trip and I stepped outside the control room to catch a break as Roc and Tim worked on their songs. It was 9:00 p.m. Suddenly, the elevator arrived.

Dan Schutte chimed in. "I was lying on the floor of the vestibule, resting up from our sessions. The elevator door opened, and the other studio's owner burst out with two police officers! I leapt to my feet. 'Good evening, officers.' And one of them said matter-of-factly, 'We have a warrant for the arrest of Erich Sylvester.'"

"The owner was obviously upset that we took the project away from his studio," Dufford continued. "They confiscated the tapes and hauled Erich away!

"So, Roc, Tim, Dan and I looked at our watches and realized it was time to pick up John from the airport. We greeted him there and I said, 'John, I have some good news and some bad news.'

"John said, 'What's the good news?' And I said, 'We got more tracks done.'

"'And what's the bad news?' And I told him, 'Erich was arrested and the tapes have been confiscated.'

"And John shook his head and said, 'I was afraid something like this might happen.'"

Sylvester explained, "I didn't actually spend time in jail. I called a lawyer friend who came over and got me out right away."

Unknown to the St. Louis Jesuits, Bruno stopped payment on the check to the original studio, and that's what got the owner upset. But Bruno and Sylvester later worked things out with the owner for the Jesuits to finish the album within 24 hours at the new studio. Twenty-four hours! The guys worked like mad as they watched the clock tick down to the Cinderella-like deadline.

"We were dying like flies in that studio," recalled Dufford, "working non-stop without sleep!"

And that is how the album that gave the world such peaceful classics as "I Lift My Soul" and "Like a Shepherd" was completed![11]

Gentle Night

Summertime meant studio time, and for the 1977 project someone – no one remembers who – came up with a novel idea. The St. Louis Jesuits recorded *Gentle Night*, possibly the first collection of music for Advent and Christmas by contemporary Catholic composers.

"Some of us had been writing music all along for Christmas liturgy," said John Foley. "St. Louis Jesuit compositions were always done for use at our community liturgies."

Bob Dufford remembers: "Once we knew we were going to do a Christmas album, we supplemented our older songs with new ones, like John's 'Just Begun.'"

By 1977, NALR had relocated to Phoenix and that summer the town was roasting in a record-breaking heat wave. It proved to be an amusing experience. "I know we recorded in July," Schutte recalls, "because we celebrated the Feast of Saint Ignatius on July 31 with the Jesuit community at Brophy Prep College in Phoenix, where we were staying."

They recorded at Pantheon Studio in Paradise Valley, west of Scottsdale, Arizona. Dennis Alexander owned Pantheon and served as engineer for *Gentle Night*. Alexander took great care to set up a Christmas mood in the studio.

Bob Dufford remembers spraying snow on the windows. Roc O'Connor recalls a small Christmas tree in the control room. Tim Manion can still picture Christmas lights strung up in the recording studio. Dan Schutte said, "Walking into the Pantheon from 113-degree heat was like walking into another world where we happened to be singing about Christmas."

"It was hilarious," John Foley recalled. "I remember taking a break outside when one of the other guys was mixing his piece. What a shock! I could almost not breathe in that outdoor furnace, so I fled back inside to Christmas."[12]

Gentle Night was Grammy-nominated and became a favorite Christmas album for many families and religious communities. Songs like "Patience, People," "Wake from Your Sleep," "A Time Will Come for Singing," and "Children, Run Joyfully" are still sung at Advent and Christmas liturgies today.

Wood Hath Hope

The year 1978 brought a different kind of project: a John Foley solo album. "We had published one collection per year for at least three years," Foley explained,

> and that year the guys were tired and not willing to put in the work for another summer project. But I had been particularly productive in those years, for whatever reason, and had a good number of pieces that had not made it on to a St. Louis Jesuits album: 'One Bread, One Body,' 'Glory to God,' 'Come to the Water,' and 'The Cry of the Poor,' to mention a few. So, I suggested that I could put out an album of just my own songs—with the help of the other guys at crucial moments. They agreed and we coordinated schedules for that Spring.
>
> Bob Dufford came down to Phoenix, and he arranged the entire orchestral accompaniment for the *Gloria*. Bob also provided the finger snaps on the title track – perhaps an experiment that had gone too far! "The other men also came down, for a short time. So, it was a St. Louis Jesuits album, even though all the songs were mine."[13]

Erich Sylvester remembered,

> John asked me at that point to let him be his own producer. By this time the Jesuits had learned so much about the studio, but we still worked very much like a team. We made notes during tracking and talked to each other as we were mixing, bringing the faders up and down at agreed upon moments. Our mixes became quite intricate.[14]

The songs on *Wood Hath Hope* turned out to be among John Foley's most enduring. His majestic setting of the "Glory to God" helped to popularize the antiphonal format (repeated refrain) for the lengthy Mass text that, with the Collect, concludes the Entrance rite of the eucharistic liturgy.

Lord of Light

Roc O'Connor gives an overview of *Lord of Light,* an album that featured some of the most beloved songs in the St. Louis Jesuit repertoire:

> The time frame when we put together *Lord of Light* is significant. We had recorded *Gentle Night* in Phoenix during the summer of 1977. Schutte and I had just finished our first year of theology at the Jesuit School of Theology in Berkeley (JSTB). Tim was either newly married or soon to be married. Duff taught math at Creighton Prep. John was working with a mentor in Toronto to gain facility in composing for classical orchestra.
>
> Recording in St. Louis during the summer of 1980, we re-connected with Kent Kesterson, the engineer in whose basement we had recorded most of *Neither Silver Nor Gold.* John and Tim had visited him at his newly formed Earth City Studios and found it to be an excellent place to record.
>
> As I recall, Dan composed 'Here I Am, Lord' for the diaconate ordinations of the Jesuits in the class just behind ours. It would have been November, 1979. It really spoke to our hearts then, as it does now. Dan composed "Only This I Want" while he was teaching at Red Cloud school on the Pine Ridge Reservation, South Dakota, in 1976. We sang it at Berkeley. Foley's piano part helped set it off as a piece for contemplation.
>
> Dan composed 'City of God' in response to a request by the late Jesuit Father Ed Maletesta, director of Jesuit *tertians* (those in preparation for final vows). A concert was planned to support the efforts of Saint Anthony Foundation food kitchen in the Tenderloin district of San Francisco. The idea was to catch folks coming out of Macy's and other stores as they shopped for Christmas.
>
> Tim's piece, 'This Alone,' was a revelation. It opens my spirit still. I probably had heard Duff's pieces, 'All the Ends of the Earth' and 'Save Us, O Lord,' while giving liturgy workshops with him. I was impressed with their strong beat and driving rhythms. Gut-driven music for sure!
>
> The real surprises for me were the songs John brought. 'Redeemer Lord' is epic. It's like nothing I've ever heard in liturgical music – so deeply existential, naming our resistances, naming our cry for God to act in the midst of the refrain, 'My shepherd is the Lord...' with the wrenching and consoling string parts! 'May We Praise You' was another revelation – its impressionistic harmonies, its simple yet piercingly lovely verses. Prayer itself.
>
> At the very darkest hour of my life up until that point, 'Jesus the Lord' was given to me. And there it was, whole: lyrics, chords, melody, the feel. A total gift.
>
> I had been learning about the 'Jesus Prayer' as a form of meditation. That certainly influenced my choice of prayerful *largo* tempo. It's all about breathing in and out with the Holy Name. I recall playing it for the others in St. Louis at the home of Tim's parents.

Foley invited the four of us to join him in Toronto during the summer of 1978 to work on music. I spent most of my time studying the Gospel of John. It was around that time when 'We Are the Champions' by Queen appeared with its majestic drum intro. I recall walking around the neighborhood where we stayed just feeling that beat, its intensity, its grandeur. After an hour or two, words began to form around the beat – 'Lift up your hearts to the Lord...' I rushed back to my room to find that Scripture, Psalm 66.

I want to recognize the amazing art our colleague and friend, Donald-David Fehrenbach, created for the cover. It portrays the light and the shadows, the glory and suffering in the paschal mystery. There's some irony in that this is the last cover Donald painted specifically for one of our covers before he died, and gives some insight into how the glory of God moved in his life.

I am so proud of this collection, especially for the way the songs have served the prayer of the Church for nearly 30 years.[15]

Seattle

It had been almost a decade since the composers that came to be known as the St. Louis Jesuits started filling the chapel at Fusz Memorial. Their journey together was an unexpected blessing but, "There was a part of each person wanting to be more expressive in his own right and, in a sense, have a little less oversight," O'Connor remembered.[16]

For several months, an idea was being discussed among themselves: Bob, Dan, Roc, and Tim would pursue formal studies in music to complement their experience and natural talent. John needed concentrated time to work on his dream orchestral project, a monumental oratorio called *Book of Glory*. "The timing was significant," Schutte recalled. "Roc and I were finishing up our theology studies in Berkeley. So, it was a transition time for the two of us. If we waited any longer he and I would be assigned to full-time ministry someplace within our provinces. And once you get rooted in those ministries then it's really hard to break free:

> John was the only one of the group who had formal music training. The rest of us had always felt the need for an opportunity to go off and do some formal music study of theory, harmony, counterpoint, and all that. Our provinces right away were supportive of the idea. We looked into Seattle University, a Jesuit institution. Father Kevin Waters, a Jesuit with a doctoral degree in music composition, was head of their music department. He graciously said, 'Come. We'll work something out.'[17]

Schutte described the program that Father Waters designed for them:

> We took classes in the music department from Kevin and other professors, in the midst of other music students. Roc, Duff, Tim, and I also had a private music class that Kevin taught us himself. Kevin would give us an exercise to

do. We'd have the class early in the week and then, on Thursday or Friday, each of us would meet individually with him to go over this exercise. And he would comb through it with us and see what we had done, and offer suggestions and say, 'This is good, that is not good. Go back and rework it.' Kevin was a gentle and kind man and was patient with all of us.[18]

Father Waters shared his thoughts about working with his renowned students.

An instructor learns early that one can only teach a few things to one's students, whether they are gifted or ordinary. One will always be on the outside and able to only 'proofread' what was written and offer tips on fundamental techniques. I vividly recall that I intended that Bob, Dan, Roc, and Tim write a lot of exercises to loosen up their compositional joints. They resisted. They were reluctant to waste time and wanted to get right down to writing a finished product. Very few genuine exercises ever got on paper during the time the group spent with me, but a few notable compositions emerged and I believe were eventually performed, published, and recorded.[19]

"Our years in Seattle were wonderful in many ways. We did some campus ministry during that time," said Schutte.

The group of us sponsored a Sunday evening liturgy with students, as a workshop to teach them about liturgy. We had a weekly planning team. There was a whole group of students who were part of the music group. It was a practicum for students that allowed them to learn how to do liturgy with us.[20]

"Developing our relationships in the group was part of our reason for going to Seattle," said O'Connor. "We decided that in order to work as a group, we were going to have to work on communicating better. We spent many hours talking about who we were and trying to relate to each other."[21]

"We had a small community house that we rented, and John, Roc, Duff, and I lived together," Schutte recalled. "Tim and his wife Trish rented another house. So, we were all there together."[22]

Father Waters designed a course of study that was essentially a master's program that could lead to a doctorate. Although Schutte was grateful for this opportunity to deepen his knowledge of music, he opted to leave the program after two years. He was anxious to get back into ministry, and had no desire for an academic career in teaching. Instead, he moved to Milwaukee to work in liturgy and campus ministry with the students at Marquette University.

O'Connor reflected on Schutte's departure:

Even when Dan moved to Marquette in 1982, while the rest of us stayed in Seattle, we wrote letters every month or so, summaries of what was going on, just to keep our communication going. Then, in the summer of 1983, John went to tertianship in Spokane, Duff came to Creighton, I went to Mankato, and Tim stayed in Seattle. We kept writing letters, and in January 1984, we came back for a meeting to see what the next step was. Tim said he didn't want to be part of the group anymore, that he didn't want to continue with music. We were blown away. It was hard.[23]

"For me, the time at the end was important," said Manion. "I decided to move away from living that life of being part of the group. There were elements that weren't working for me anymore. The biggest element was me. Ultimately, my spirituality was changing."[24]

"My responsibility in changing the dynamics of the St. Louis Jesuits haunted me in 1980," said Father Waters:

> Would this group, which had a unified style and approach to music, be altered radically by the workshop? Would the individuality of each composer come to the fore in such a way that the distinctive style of the group began to fade or even disappear? I do not believe I can answer these questions now. But perhaps the questions have changed or, perhaps they no longer matter.[25]

Certainly, the Seattle years inspired the group's productivity as composers. John, Bob, Dan, and Roc realized that when they pooled their songs together they had more than enough for a new collection. Even though Tim was no longer with them, they decided to record an album of 22 songs entitled *The Steadfast Love*. This 1985 collaboration was reviewed in *Worship* magazine.

> These are 22 songs from the well-established group that has been a hallmark in American musical liturgy for 15 years. This edition features four of the standard members: John Foley, Bob Dufford, Roc O'Connor, and Dan Schutte — all Jesuits. Tim Manion, long associated with the band, is not included among the composer/lyricists. However, the stylistic consistency is the same, with generally excellent attention to liturgical appropriateness and lyrical prayerfulness. [26]

The Steadfast Love is perhaps the most underappreciated album by the St. Louis Jesuits. It deserves a fresh listening, as it reveals how their years of study in Seattle affected their songwriting and studio craft. Interestingly, for the first time, they shared lead vocal duties with several people outside the group, including an up-and-coming Minnesota composer named David Haas.

"I got to know John when he came to Saint Paul and visited with Michael Joncas, Marty Haugen and me," Haas remembered.

> And he invited me to come out to Omaha for the *Steadfast Love* sessions. I think the St. Louis Jesuits wanted to break out of the box with that album. They never had other soloists before and suddenly they did. They had female lead vocalists, and I sang on John's 'The Christ of God' and Roc's 'How Glorious Your Name.' What an honor![27]

In retrospect, *The Steadfast Love* may have been a subliminal expression of upcoming changes in the St. Louis Jesuits. O'Connor reflected on this:

At the beginning of the summer of 1986, about a week before we were to begin tertianship, Dan and I had lunch. He told me he'd been struggling a lot. He said that he'd decided to leave the Society. This was quite a surprise. The experience of that was hard, especially after having had these times of getting together and making commitments to each other. These hard times strained our relationships.[28]

"It was the most difficult decision I have ever made," said Schutte. "It wasn't that I was angry at the Society or didn't love the priesthood; there was a need for intimacy in my life that was so strong that I knew I would be losing myself if I did not pay attention to it."[29]

"Discernment" is an inadequate word that describes the process of finding out God's will through prayer, Scripture, spiritual direction, and the events that are unfolding in one's life. At a very young age, John, Bob, Roc, Dan, and Tim each discerned a call to join the Society of Jesus. After the surprise success of *Neither Silver Nor Gold*, they discerned a group calling as liturgical composers. Several fulfilling years later, it seemed that God was now calling them to follow individual paths.

"One of the good aspects of our separation was that people went on to discover their own style and voice," said O'Connor. "We explored what it means to compose in the Church's life and in the mid-1980s and early 1990s. The goal was to grow in the knowledge and the craft of composition, and each of us went in different paths along those lines."[30]

"We never talked about it as being an ending as much as 'let's just see,'" said Schutte.[31]

"After you've been working together for 12 or 14 years, it's hard to keep doing the same music," said Foley. "People had their own interests. It was tough leaving but I am sure it was the best thing to do. We toasted one another, went our separate ways, and remained friends."[32]

Bob Dufford became a successful spiritual director, working for many years as retreat director and composer-in-residence at the Jesuit Retreat House at Oshkosh, Wisconsin. He enjoys doing orchestral arranging and is working on a new collection of meditative music for prayer and contemplation.

John Foley continued his studies in music and composed many orchestral works, including *Book of Glory* (1981), *Dance of Life* (1983), and *Like Winter Waiting* (2000). He also established three important liturgical programs affiliated with Saint Louis University: the Liturgical Composers Forum, the Center for Liturgy, and the Sunday Website.[33] He also wrote *Creativity and the Roots of Liturgy* (Pastoral Press).

Tim Manion recorded a solo liturgical album – *There Is a River* – and then pursued a career related to his love for the great outdoors.

Roc O'Connor received master's degrees in sacred theology, biblical theology, and liturgical studies, and taught Eucharist and Sacraments in the Theology Department at Creighton University. He has also served as rector of the Jesuit Community at

Creighton. He has written articles for magazines and journals and has published a book on liturgical theology, *In the Midst of Our Storms.*

Dan Schutte went on to a prolific career as a liturgical composer, with more than 14 solo collections of songs that have become standards in the contemporary liturgical repertoire. He has served as composer-in-residence at the University of San Francisco, and is in much demand as a workshop presenter at parishes and national conferences.

Throughout their career as a group, the St. Louis Jesuits recorded new songs in the summertime during a break in their ministerial or academic commitments. People who loved their music wondered if another creative summer would ever happen again for these respected composers who had blessed the Church so abundantly with their gifts of song. It would be a 20-year wait, but their storied collaboration would eventually return one more time.

[1] An insider's Berkeley joke, as documented by King, Andrew David, editor, *Berkeley Poetry Review,* Issue 43 (2016).

[2] Gale, Mike, editor, *The St. Louis Jesuits: Thirty Years* (Portland, OR, Oregon Catholic Press, 2006) 98.

[3] Canedo, Ken, *Keep the Fire Burning: The Folk Mass Revolution* (Portland, OR: Pastoral Press, 2009) 107.

[4] Interview with the author, September 1, 2014 in San Francisco.

[5] McDermott, S.J., Jim, "Sing a New Song," *America: The National Catholic Review.* May 23, 2005.

[6] Canedo, Ken, liner notes for *Earthen Vessels: 40th Anniversary Edition* (OCP, 2015).

[7] Interview with the author, September 1, 2014 in San Francisco.

[8] Interview with the author, May 4, 2017 in Portland, OR.

[9] Interview with the author, September 15, 2015 in Milwaukee, Wisconsin.

[10] Interview with the author, April 2009, for CD release of *Neither Silver Nor Gold.*

[11] Story compiled from three separate interviews with the author: Bob Dufford, May 4, 2017 in Portland, OR; Erich Sylvester, June 19, 2017 in San Francisco, CA; and Dan Schutte, November 3, 2017, via email. And yes, the owner of the studio shall remain nameless.

[12] Canedo, Ken, liner notes for *Gentle Night: 40th Anniversary Edition* (OCP, 2017).

[13] Interview with the author, October 13, 2017 via email from St. Louis, Missouri.

[14] Interview with the author, June 19, 2017 in San Francisco, California.

[15] Interview with the author, October 23, 2017, via email from Milwaukee, Wisconsin.

[16] McDermott, S.J., Jim, "Sing a New Song," *America: The National Catholic Review.* May 30, 2005.

[17] Interview with the author, September 1, 2014 in San Francisco, California.

[18] Interview with the author, September 1, 2014 in San Francisco, California.

[19] Gale, Mike, editor, *The St. Louis Jesuits: Thirty Years* (Portland, OR, Oregon Catholic Press, 2006) 81.

[20] Interview with the author, September 1, 2014 in San Francisco, California.

[21] Gale, Mike, editor, *The St. Louis Jesuits: Thirty Years* (Portland, OR, Oregon Catholic Press, 2006) 121.

[22] Interview with the author, September 1, 2014 in San Francisco, California.

[23] Gale, Mike, editor, *The St. Louis Jesuits: Thirty Years* (Portland, OR, Oregon Catholic Press, 2006) 121.

[24] Gale, Mike, editor, *The St. Louis Jesuits: Thirty Years* (Portland, OR, Oregon Catholic Press, 2006) 112.

[25] Gale, Mike, editor, *The St. Louis Jesuits: Thirty Years* (Portland, OR, Oregon Catholic Press, 2006) 81.

[26] Mckenna, SJ, Edward, Worship, Vol. 60, No. 3, May 1986.

[27] Interview with the author, September 9, 2017, in Portland, Oregon.

[28] Gale, Mike, editor, *The St. Louis Jesuits: Thirty Years* (Portland, OR, Oregon Catholic Press, 2006) 121.

[29] McDermott, S.J., Jim, "Sing a New Song," *America: The National Catholic Review.* May 30, 2005.

[30] Gale, Mike, editor, *The St. Louis Jesuits: Thirty Years* (Portland, OR, Oregon Catholic Press, 2006) 121.

[31] McDermott, S.J., Jim, "Sing a New Song," *America: The National Catholic Review.* May 30, 2005.

[32] Gale, Mike, editor, *The St. Louis Jesuits: Thirty Years* (Portland, OR, Oregon Catholic Press, 2006) 102.

[33] The Sunday Website can be found at www.liturgy.slu.edu

Bob Fabing, SJ

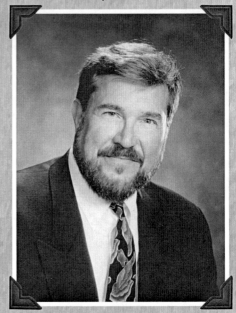

Ray Bruno

Marty Haugen, David Haas and Michael Joncas

The Dameans

Fr. Virgil Funk

Grayson Warren Brown

John Michael Talbot

Gregory Norbet

Cary Landry & Carol Jean Kinghorn

Erich Sylvester

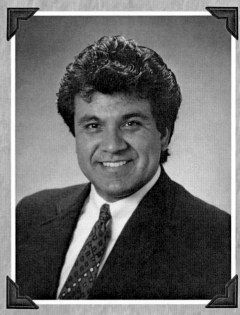

Pedro Rubalcava

Mary Frances Reza

Bob Hurd

Tom Kendzia

St. Louis Jesuits

Chapter Seven

"Misa Panamericana"
Spanish Liturgical Music

Nothing so defines a people as its music. The sounds of diversity of the Hispanic community are easily heard. The differences of rhythm, melodies, and style reveals us to ourselves and to one another.

-Arturo J. Pérez[1]

The spirit of these songs does not apply to a single generation, and each proclaims a permanent message to the Church, defining the pastoral guidelines – a people called to be evangelizers, missionaries and lovers of justice... These songs, popular in many countries, have no national boundaries and move freely between cultures.

-Mary Frances Reza[2]

¿Cómo no vamos a cantar si nuestro corazón está de fiesta? [How can we *not* sing if our hearts are so full of joy?]

-Monsignor Cesáreo Gabaráin, composer and pastor[3]

The demographics of Southern California were rapidly changing in the 1950s. In Los Angeles the families of European descent had settled in the suburbs as World War II veterans took advantage of the G.I. Bill.[4] But there was a gradual shift in the older neighborhoods, with immigrants settling in from the Philippines, Indonesia, and Latin America – particularly from Mexico. One began to overhear Spanish conversations in the grocery stores, and street vendors sold ethnic foods from their wheeled carts. *Panaderías* (bakeries) sprang up everywhere.

Los Angeles, seemingly overnight, had become a multicultural mecca. Certainly, there were some tensions between ethnic communities, but the children of this era went to school and played with friends of all backgrounds. Unfortunately, one social institution lagged behind in acceptance of this changing demographic: the local Catholic parish.

On L.A.'s westside, a certain pastor ran his parish like a tight ship. Born in Los Angeles of an Irish family, Father had witnessed tremendous change in the Church since he began his pastorate in 1960, and he grudgingly accepted the change in the liturgy from Latin to English with cautious hesitation. He forbade the playing of guitars at Mass. He was bewildered by the growing number of Hispanics who came to Mass on Sunday, and he resisted the requests to begin a Spanish Mass. "When people come to America," he often groused, "they need to speak English."

But Father made one exception to his English-only policy. The church parking lot was getting full on the weekends, and traffic became a nightmare between Masses. His solution was to place a hand-painted sign high above one of the parking lot gates: "¡*Sólo Salida!* – Exit Only!"

The subliminal message to the Hispanic community was very damaging, but a new pastor was more open, and began a Spanish Mass at 12:00 p.m. every Sunday. The church was immediately filled to overflowing at this noon liturgy, and the lively participation of the Hispanic community, especially in music, was an inspiration to the whole parish.[5] This dynamic was happening in major cities across the United States. Timothy Matovina, professor of theology and executive director of the Institute for Latino Studies at the University of Notre Dame, noted how the changing demographics are affecting the Catholic Church.

> Catholics comprise the largest religious group in the United States, encompassing nearly a fourth of all US residents. Hispanics constitute more than a third of US Catholics. They are the reason why Catholicism is holding its own relative to other religions in the United States. And given the relative youthfulness of the Latino community, Hispanic Catholics will continue to represent an increasing percentage of US Catholics over time.[6]

As the Spanish Mass proliferated, it soon became apparent that this new liturgy was more than just a proclamation by the priest of the ritual texts in the Spanish language. The level of participation by the assembly was often more animated and engaging. Raúl R. Gómez from the Sacred Heart School of Theology at Hales Corners, Wisconsin, made the following observation.

> The liturgy is the first place where Hispanics/Latinos in the United States meet the Church and enter into its life... At liturgy Hispanics/Latinos find their faith confirmed and their identity as Catholic believers nourished. This leads them to bring their faith expressions to the celebration of the sacraments and the Eucharist. In those parishes receptive to this, oftentimes there is lack of standing room available for Hispanics/Latinos hungry to satisfy their spiritual needs.

> I believe the Spanish Mass is so full because the pastor has provided a welcome to the community that does not criticize or diminish its faith expressions. As a consequence, the Hispanic/Latino parishioners have begun to take responsibility for the welfare and life of the parish. I contend the liturgy has been the catalyst for this result.[7]

This engaged level of Hispanic/Latino participation in the liturgy is expressed most especially in the music. But before we get into a discussion on the music itself, it is important to understand the place of popular devotion in Hispanic Catholic spirituality.

Prior to the Second Vatican Council, American Catholics of European descent had many devotions that were not connected with the Mass. After the changeover to the

English liturgy, these devotions waned as emphasis was placed on the celebration of the Eucharist, "the source and summit of the Christian life."[8] The apparent North American tension between the official eucharistic liturgy and popular devotion – popular religiosity – was not a concern for Hispanic Catholics. Arturo J. Pérez, a leading Latino liturgist, offers some definitions.

> Popular religiosity is the ritual expression of the spiritual life of the Hispanic people. It is an expression of how the Hispanic community belongs to the Church. In conjunction with official worship, the faith life of the community is nourished through these devotions.

> Within popular religiosity are contained the symbols and rituals that are accepted as the right/rite way of celebrating a birth, joining two persons in marriage, bringing our beloved dead to their final place of rest, as well as initiating young women into the community through *Quinceañera* (15th birthday) celebration, protecting our children from evil through blessings, and acting out our prayer through promises and processions. In many instances, these practices perform a sacramental function in the eyes of the Hispanic family.[9]

Raúl Gómez notes that "since the beginning, Christianity was able to present a unique way of universalizing people without destroying their identities so they would not have to disappear either through assimilation or marginalization. One way it was able to accomplish this was through the interweaving of the Christian message with local traditions."[10]

The Hispanic community has a rich tradition of praying through popular devotions both at home and in the streets. Many of these traditions are tied to feast days celebrated throughout the year. During Advent the *posadas* reenact the pilgrimage of Mary and Joseph on their way to Bethlehem in a novena celebration that goes from home to home.[11] Matovina explained:

> The *posada* reminds us that our joy is not complete until we receive the rejected and forgotten in our lives. Similarly, when Hispanics place the child Jesus in the crib *(acostada del niño),* offer their devotion at the manger scene *(nacimiento)* or recall the worship of the shepherds in a Christmas drama *(la pasterrela),* they encounter a human Jesus who is tangible and approachable.[12]

Lent brings Ash Wednesday and overcrowded churches, including people who might miss regular Sunday liturgy. On Good Friday, there are elaborate passion pageants in the streets. "What matters on Good Friday is faithful accompaniment," Matovina observed. "Mary and Jesus walk together in their hour of gravest need while participants ritually imitate what mother and son did at the first Way of the Cross in Jerusalem."[13]

El Dia de los Muertos (The Day of the Dead) in November has recently become adopted in a misunderstood way among non-Hispanics because of increasing commercialization. "It is a time to honor and communicate with our dead," explains Lara

Medina, an expert on Chicano and indigenous American religious practices. "Among indigenous Indians, it was seen as a very privileged time when the divide between the physical and spiritual worlds dissolved, and the spirits can return for all that is laid out for them." Hence, the custom of family meals at the cemetery.[14]

Among the many aspects of popular religiosity, the most beloved among Hispanics is devotion to Mary. For the Mexican community, this culminates with the Feast of Our Lady of Guadalupe on December 12. The celebration begins in the early morning with *las mañanitas* (morning songs), along with flowers, prayers, Scripture readings and tributes to the Blessed Virgin as she appeared to the humble Juan Diego at Tepeyac. This often leads to the celebration of Mass, during which there might be a dramatic reenactment of the apparition story. Matovina reflected on the meaning and importance of this celebration.

> Like Juan Diego, numerous Hispanic devotees have stinging memories of being ignored or rejected. They have met polite disdain or outright hostility in their dealings with sales clerks, bosses, coworkers, teachers, police officers, health care providers, social workers, government employees, professional colleagues, and even fellow Catholic parishioners and leaders. Thus, it is not surprising that devotees resonate with the liturgical drama of the lowly Juan Diego's rejection, his encounter with a loving mother, his calling to be Guadalupe's chosen messenger, his unwavering faith, and his final vindication as an unexpected hero. Devotees ardently attest that Guadalupe uplifts and strengthens them as she did with Juan Diego.[15]

Other Latin-American countries have their own devotions to a Marian image, including Nuestra Señora de Lujan (Argentina), Nuestra Señora del Carmen (Colombia), Nuestra Señora del Cobre (Cuba), Nuestra Señora de la Altagracia (Dominican Republic), and Nuestra Señora de la Providencia (Puerto Rico).

Of this rich tapestry of liturgy and private devotion, Father Juan Sosa made the following observation:

> Eucharist and the popular piety of the faithful seem to stand as two complimentary—not contradictory—forms of spiritual nourishment for the faithful, particularly among Hispanic Catholics.[16]

This brief survey of the pastoral theology of the Hispanic Catholic community in the United States helps us to understand better the importance of the music that accompanies these many celebrations. Father Sosa reflected on this:

> The joy of being Church, coupled with a personal experience of conversion, allows many of our Hispanic Catholics to join their voices in praising God, whose mercy and whose love they continually experience. Music, as a symbol and as a language, translates the rough moments of human experience into a sacrificial offering of self with Jesus at his banquet of love.[17]

Composer Mary Frances Reza grew up in Dawson, New Mexico, where her mother Amelia López García served as organist and choir director at Saint John the Baptist Church. Mary Frances remembers singing at her parish church as a child. "Throughout the world where Spanish was spoken, the homily and music were in Spanish, while the rest of the Mass was in Latin. That was the same pattern in the United States. And we had our Spanish hymnals." [18] Many of the early hymnals have become family heirlooms.

> Perhaps the first hymnal of the Spanish-speaking community was published by the *Revista Católica* (Las Vegas, New Mexico) in the 1900s as a blue book called *Cánticos espirituales*. It consisted mostly of music from Spain but also included popular religious hymns. This little book would be the staple of religious musical nourishment of the New Mexican family and community.[19]

Pedro Rubalcava, liturgical composer and music development and outreach director at OCP, was a child when the Mass opened up to the vernacular languages in 1964. He grew up at Our Lady of Perpetual Help Church in Brawley, California.

> I distinctly remember going to Mass before I was 6 years old and the songs were in Latin. I remember my father José had his missal and it was in Latin and Spanish, side-by-side. When the Mass started to be celebrated in Spanish my father was in the Holy Name Society. Most of the men were ushers but my father was a lector.

> Our parish was 99.9% Mexican or Mexican-American. I was still in grade school when the change came in the renewal of the liturgy. Our parish had two Masses in Spanish and two Masses in English. Most of our songs were devotional, like *'Cantemos al Amor de los Amores,'* or *'Bendito, Bendito'* that came from Adoration of the Blessed Sacrament. My family prayed the rosary every night and we did Marian songs that we also sang at Mass.[20]

Arturo Pérez has documented those early days:

> The first attempts at developing music for the Hispanic community centered more in translating into Spanish hymns from other cultures and languages. United States and European religious music was soon being sung at Spanish Masses. In some cases, popular melodies of the day were rewritten with religious texts. In this way, the music of "Red River Valley" (appears in some areas under the title, *'Junto a ti'* and *'Una tarde en caná'*), "Michael Row the Boat Ashore" (sometimes called *'El Señor resucitó'* and *'Caridad y comprensión'*), and "O Clementine" (*'Viva Cristo Rey'* appears based on this) can still be heard at Eucharist in some parishes.[21]

"There must have been at least three hymns from Mexico that were sung to the melody of 'Blowin' in the Wind' by Bob Dylan," remembers Reza.[22] "We sang Spanish text to Joe Wise's 'Take Our Bread' and Ray Repp's 'Into Your Hands,'" recalls Rubalcava. "Then, little by little, I remember songs that came from Spain through Mexico. A lot of them were based on psalms and there were a lot of scriptural songs. I was 12 years old when I joined the parish choir."[23]

A breakthrough in music composed specifically for the liturgy arrived with the publication of a Mass setting from Cuernavaca, Mexico.

> One particular influence that inspired the composition of Mexican-American music was the publication of the *Misa Panamericana* (1965) by Juan Marcos Leclerc, who was working at the Centro de Formación Intercultural (CIF) that was founded by Ivan Illich. This Mass, a conglomeration of melodies from different Latin American countries, is popularly called *Misa Mariachi* since it was played by mariachis and was adopted for regular Sunday use at the Cathedral in Cuernavaca, Mexico, in 1966 by Bishop Sergio Mendez Arceo. This music brought Mexican and Latin American rhythms into the celebration of the Eucharist.[24]

Stylistically eclectic, *Misa Panamericana* was inspired by melodies and rhythms from Chile, Brazil, Costa Rica, Mexico, and other regions across Latin America. Mary Frances Reza recalls the story behind this landmark composition:

> Juan Marcos Leclerc was a Canadian who came to study with Ivan Illich in Cuernavaca, fell in love with the folkloric music and recognized the potential for incorporating this music style into the parts of the Mass. With the work and time involved teaching only small parts of the Mass, he decided it would take a professional group to learn the entire Mass. He called upon the music group, Mariachi Hermanos Macías. In the hierarchy of instruments, using trumpets in the church was a bigger hurdle. It was the musicians themselves who doubted the worthiness of playing the trumpet at Mass. When *Misa Panamericana* was introduced in 1966, the early opinions were divided in Mexico. Full support did not happen overnight. It took time to be accepted by everyone.[25]

As the name *"panamericana"* implies, the music of the growing Hispanic repertoire was not exclusively from Mexico. Arturo Pérez identifies at least three other regions of influence: New Mexico, Puerto Rico, and Cuba.

> The New Mexican tradition is more than a geographical place or an individual state on a map. It expresses a particular perspective within the Southwest that dates back to 1598.[26] A particularly rich musical tradition was that of the *alabados* (praises). These were praises sung to God. They are popularly believed to have originated at the time of conquest. The *alabados* were the Indian attempts to imitate the hymns and chants of the missionaries. Through song, the indigenous people learned Church doctrine.[27]

A major influence of music from this region were the seminarians from Montezuma Seminary in Las Vegas, New Mexico. As a result of the Mexican Revolution, a new constitution was adopted, providing for a secular government and prohibiting any role or influence by the Catholic Church.

During this tumultuous era, hundreds of priests were killed or disappeared, many more fled the country, and the Catholic Church was banned throughout Mexico. It was during this period of religious persecution, which continued into the 1940s, that the Catholic hierarchies of both the United States and Mexico established Montezuma as a seminary in exile.[28]

"The seminarians were enthusiastic, talented musicians who loved to sing," said Reza:

They brought the spirit of renewal to every parish they visited. They were composers and arrangers. Juan Ferneli was in charge of the music. This country was blessed by their presence and those seminarians who…continued in their ministries [after the seminary closed in 1922]. Among them were Eleazar Cortés, who eventually became an OCP composer; Pedro Ramirez (Madre Morena); and Deacon Juan Barajas Ruelas, who became director of the Hispanic office in the Archdiocese of Santa Fe. They compiled a hymnal in 1972, *Montezuma en la Eucaristía,* as a farewell memorial to take with them to their new destinations.[29]

"We had the privilege of coming to know Cesário Gabaráin, the composer from Spain, long before OCP introduced him at NPM in Long Beach, California," (1989) remembers Reza.

One of the most influential aspects of liturgical life from New Mexico lies in the impact of various publications. In addition to the aforementioned *Cánticos espirituales* hymnal of the early 1900s, the Penitentes, a Catholic brotherhood from this region, had their own hymnal, *Himnos sagrados* (1912). The Oblates of Mary Immaculate also compiled *Tesoro de cánticos sagrados* (1953). And in 1966, Henry J. Rael published what is considered the very first Spanish missalette, *El misalito: Canta el pueblo de Dios.* Published by his own company, SIMCO (San Ignacio Music Co.), *El misalito* was designed to foster the people's participation by putting the liturgical texts and songs in their hands, at least ten years before J.S. Paluch published its *Misalito Parroquial.*[30]

Puerto Rico was a Spanish colony in the 15th century, and became a possession of the United States. Political exiles of the island moved to New York City in the late 19th century, and the 1920s saw the first significant wave of migration:

Puerto Ricans came to the United States in most concentrated numbers during the 1950s, a time when the United States economy needed entry-level workers, especially in the industrial and manufacturing centers of the Northeast and Midwest. Poor, unskilled migrants from the interior, known as *jíbaros,* arrived on inexpensive airplane flights from San Juan to New York City. Around 1965, the Great Migration stopped.[31]

For the music of Puerto Rico, Arturo Pérez cites three influential works.

Father William Loperena, OP, and Pedro Escabi, an Episcopal layman and musician, both of Puerto Rico, along with Angel Pérez, a Spaniard, could perhaps be recognized as the first composers of post-Vatican II Hispanic music.

Within a year after the *Constitution on the Sacred Liturgy* was published, Loperena wrote *Misa Jíbara,* the Roman Mass based on the popular rhythms of Puerto Rico. This Mass found favor within the general community while it gained criticism from the local bishops, who upheld music from Spain as the classical standard worthy for liturgy. By nature, popular rhythms strengthen identity, in this case Puerto Rican identity. The Mass was perceived as being influenced by the political liberationist movements of the day and therefore subject to suspicion.

Angel Pérez, a Spaniard who worked in the Puerto Rican community of New York in the mid-1960s, also made a contribution. As part of the Spanish-speaking Apostolate Office, Pérez wrote *Misa Hispana.* This Mass was an attempt to represent the musical styles of the many different ethnic groups of the area.

The Puerto Rican order of religious women, Instituto de Jesús Mediator, in the late sixties asked Pedro Escabí for a Mass set to Puerto Rican popular melodies. He wrote *Misa en la menor* (in A minor, a traditional tone for popular music) that would be played by guitar, cuatro, and other instruments. It was used until the early 1970s.[32]

Throughout the first half of the 20th century, the island nation of Cuba was a popular vacation destination for Americans because of its convenient location just 90 miles off the coast of southern Florida. Political turmoil in the 1930s led to the migration of Cubans, many of whom settled in the Miami area. This was intensified dramatically by Fidel Castro's rise to power in 1958, and the embargo by the US government. Whole families fled Cuba by boat over treacherous waters at great personal risk, often clinging to nothing more than their clothes, their family, and their Catholic faith. Arturo Pérez makes this observation of the liturgical music of Cuba.

> Since 1978, research on different musical styles was being done in the Miami area. Under the auspices of the Committee of Popular Piety, chaired by Father Juan Sosa, the Shrine of Our Lady of Charity, and in conjunction with the Southeast Pastoral Institute (SEPI), *Misa Cubana* was published in 1981. This would be the first of many ventures into the systemic approach of providing music in the rhythm and style of this Caribbean community. There was a growing hope that music would be more scripturally based and conform more closely to *Music in Catholic Worship.* To this end, SEPI and the Office of Worship and Spiritual Life developed programs through Barry University on music and liturgy.[33]

As with the folk tradition of any nation, music composed by and for the Hispanic community was originally shared informally by oral transmission. Formal publication was an important step forward in uniting the diverse communities, and raising the bar in skill level for local musicians involved in their parish liturgies. But, as Arturo Pérez observed, publication and national distribution had unique challenges.

Publishing for the Spanish-speaking community of the United States has been a risky business venture. Presses were hesitant to invest in an unknown and untested market. In this vacuum, scriptural texts, liturgical and homiletic aids, and music hymnals were produced on the local level. Materials were either homemade or imported from other Spanish-speaking countries. While this provided a sense of creativity, it was also frustrating in its failure to produce well-translated and appropriately sensitive cultural material for the diverse Hispanic community. Frequently, it was easier to import and copy material than to write and produce new music.[34]

One of the first published Spanish Mass settings in the United States was Harry Lojewski's *Misa de los Mariachis,* recorded and distributed in 1969 by FEL Publications. Although not Hispanic himself, Lojewski was choir director for Our Lady of Lourdes Church in Northridge, California. He eventually became vice president of MGM/United Artists, and his own background as a Hollywood composer and producer allowed him access to some of the Los Angeles area's finest studio musicians. The result was a stunning professional mariachi recording that beautifully showcased Lojewski's enchanting melodies and rhythms. *Misa de los Mariachis* became widely popular with Hispanic pastoral musicians in California, the Southwest and beyond.

Our Sunday Visitor publishing house, based in Huntington, Indiana, published one of the first national bilingual hymnals, *Cantemos al Señor/The Catholic Hymnal,* in 1975. This hymnal is remembered for its unique format: the Spanish *Cantemos* section could be flipped upside down for the English *Catholic Hymnal* section. Each contained the Order of Mass, two Latin Mass settings, and hymns from the respective language-based traditions.

In 1979, GIA Publications in Chicago released *Misa San José* by Marianist Brother Howard Hughes, a prolific liturgical composer of English hymns and psalms. The publication of this Mass setting triggered off a mountain of unsolicited Spanish-language manuscripts at GIA, which eventually published *Quiero servirte mi Señor* by Lorenzo Florián in 1981. The songs of Jacques Berthiér that were sung by the ecumenical monastic community in Taizé, France, were published in Spanish and English in 1986. And in 1988, GIA published *Alma Mía* by Donna Peña. Florían was eventually hired as an editor, and took a lead in GIA's editorial direction in their service to the Hispanic community.

After Henry Rael's *El misalito* began publication in 1966, the J.S. Paluch Company started publishing *Misalito Parroquial* in the 1970s, and it quickly became a popular resource for many parishes. It began as a supplement to the company's successful English-language *Monthly Missalette,* and the resulting dual language resource was very helpful for parishes. But the Spanish insert was limited in its number of pages, offering only a more traditional repertoire of popular religious hymns and music from composers of Spain. In recent years, *Misalito Parroquial* has grown into a larger stand-alone resource that allowed for a wider variety of composers. Paluch deepened its commitment to the Hispanic community when its music division, World Library

Publications, hired Peter Kolar in 1996. He would become the founding editor of the company's bilingual missal, *Celebremos/Let us Celebrate* and its companion music resource, *Himnario/Hymnal,* featuring songs by Pedro Rubalcava, Diego Correa and Damaris Thillet, Eleazar Cortés, and many other composers.[35]

In 1977, NALR released *Hola Dios,* a Spanish translation of selected songs from *Hi God* by Carey Landry and Carol Jean Kinghorn. In 1985, the company released *Love the Lord Your God...Con Todo El Corazón* by Al Valverde and Vic Cabrera and, in 1988, *Amanecer* by Peter (Pedro) Rubalcava. This album was nominated for a Grammy in the Best Mexican-American Performance category in 1990.

Of all the established liturgical publishers, Oregon Catholic Press made the biggest early commitment to serve the Hispanic church. As Arturo Pérez observed, "No publishing house has done more to influence Hispanic music than OCP." [36] Composer M.D. Ridge documented the story behind the company's groundbreaking Spanish-language hymnal, *Cánticos:*

> The first Spanish hymnal published by OCP Publications, was a slim paperback volume called *Cánticos de Gracias y Alabanza,* published in 1982. A Spanish language insert in the music section of *Today's Missal* had been offered since 1978. Fritz Meagher, then OCP's publisher, and Owen Alstott, publisher from 1983-1992, believed that the Spanish music section was too limited in the amount of music it could provide; a Spanish language hymnal was needed to serve Hispanic and bilingual communities. *Cánticos* was the result—the first Spanish hymnal by a major Catholic publisher in the United States. A local director, Mary Lovell, helped Alstott put together a core repertoire of music used in the area. Like an ethnomusicologist, Alstott went from service to service with a tape recorder, recording the songs being used and subsequently transcribing them into standard notation.
>
> Honesto Badilla, a priest of the Diocese of San Bernardino, had amassed an enormous personal collection of books of Spanish liturgical music. When he heard of OCP's project, he invited Alstott to come to California to research his library.
>
> When the songs were chosen, there was a long search for the owners of copyrighted material. There was a strong emphasis on traditional folk tunes – the "people's music." The hymnal contained 215 selections; over half were traditional. *Cánticos* was published in two editions: words and melody line, and words only. The accompaniment manual was for guitar, the primary instrument of Hispanic liturgies at that time. Four cassette tapes containing 70 songs were also offered so that musicians of an oral culture could learn the songs.[37]

The 1982 release of *Cánticos* was well timed because that was the year that the Southwest Liturgical Conference (SWLC)[38] was meeting in Albuquerque, New Mexico. The conference theme was "Hispanic Worship," and Mary Frances Reza, who served as Coordinator of Liturgies and Music, remembers the excitement among the participants for the new resource. Reza continues:

> People in the exhibit area were telling each other, 'Did you see the new *himnario?*' They were excited because even though we've had other Spanish hymnals available in the United States long before *Cánticos,* this was the first time that a major Catholic publisher was distributing a resource of this scope throughout the country.

> Owen and I had a meeting and he listened with excitement when I let him know there was a renaissance of liturgical music composed by American Hispanic composers. He asked, 'Do you think we should publish another Spanish hymnal?' My response, of course, was 'Yes' and he requested my help for this new project. Songs began pouring in to OCP from around the country. Some were words-only with cassettes; other were notated.[39]

Paulette McCoy and the OCP staff in Portland worked tirelessly on a project never tackled before. They spent many long hours across several months transcribing, editing and recording songs, and seeking the necessary permissions. The fruit of this labor of love was *Flor y Canto,* published in 1989, and as of this writing, is now in its third edition.

There were several other spiritual movements in the United States that greatly influenced Hispanic ministry, both in music and in leadership empowerment. The Charismatic Renewal, whose origin in the United States was covered in chapter two, brought accessible and appealing songs of praise from the evangelical church to the Catholic repertoire. The Cursillo movement was also influential, and will be discussed in the next chapter. But the story of Hispanic music ministry would not be complete without a discussion on *Encuentro.*

In the late 1960s and early 1970s, parishes in the United States saw their numbers rise significantly after including a Spanish Mass in their weekend schedule. The subsequent increase of involvement of the Hispanic community at liturgy and in the life of the parish was a blessing to the Church. In 1972, the United States Bishops convened the *Encuentro Nacional Hispano de Pastoral* to give official recognition to the growing Hispanic presence in dioceses across America.

What exactly is *Encuentro?* Here is a description from the United States Conference of Catholic Bishops:

> *Encuentro*[40] is a two-year process of missionary activity, consultation, leadership development and pastoral discernment in parishes, dioceses and episcopal regions that culminates in a national event. A primary outcome of the *Encuentro* process is to discern pastoral practices and priorities to impact the quality of ministry among Hispanic/Latino Catholics under the leadership of US bishops.[41]

"Because of the growth in numbers, the US Bishops and grassroots leadership discerned a calling from within the Church itself," says Pedro Rubalcava. "It was also connected to what was going on in the secular world, to education and discrimination. The Church started taking a look at who we are as Church to develop leadership and to inspire more vocations to the priesthood to serve the growing Latino community.

"I remember as a teenager going with my dad to the first *Encuentro* meetings that were happening at our parish. Someone from the diocese would come and that was very impressive because we were in the Imperial Valley which, at that time, was considered a forgotten part of the Diocese of San Diego."[42]

Local leaders were chosen to represent their parish concerns at a diocesan gathering. Diocesan leaders shared their discussions at a regional gathering. And finally, those pastoral regions sent representatives to the national gathering. That first national *Encuentro* was held at Trinity College in Washington, DC, on June 19-22, 1972. More than 250 people participated, including eight bishops, 130 priests, 54 women religious, 2 men religious, 15 laywomen, and 42 laymen. Three conclusions resulted from this national *Encuentro*:

1. There must be greater participation of the Spanish speaking in leadership;
2. Regional pastoral centers, coordinated nationally, should be established;
3. We Spanish-speaking American Catholics are impelled by the Spirit to share responsibility for the growth of the kingdom among our people and all peoples of our country.

This initial *Encuentro* called for a national episcopal committee for the Spanish speaking, the establishment of a Secretariat (a division for the Spanish-speaking), and the establishment of pastoral institutes.[43] It also focused on issues affecting Hispanics at the national, regional, and diocesan levels, *Comunidades Eclesiales de Base* (Basic Church Communities movement), ministry, lay postulate, liturgy, religious education and catechetics, Catholic schools, and the social and economic challenges of the time.[44]

Post-*Encuentro*, the bishops, clergy, and lay and religious leaders were sent home to implement these conclusions on the regional, diocesan, and parish levels. *Encuentro* has reconvened on a fairly regular basis through the years, and each has brought more participants, more empowerment, and more effective change. At this writing, *Encuentro* is now in the midst of its fifth gathering.

Music is an important part of *Encuentro,* because gatherings at every level involve prayer services and the celebration of the Eucharist. Mary Frances Reza has fond memories of enthusiastic busloads of choirs, musicians and leaders, meeting fellow music ministers and leaders from around the country, and learning each other's songs. She reflected on this experience:

> To help with the process of music selection, a survey was taken to identify the songs familiar to those who would be participating at the regional *Encuentro*. A similar poll was taken for the national *Encuentro*. Members of the Instituto

Nacional Hispano de Liturgia surveyed their regions and submitted song lists. It was interesting to see the consistency in the regions' lists.

Songs like *"Un Pueblo Que Camina"* (Emilio Vicente Matéu), *"Iglesia Peregrina"* (Cesáreo Gabaráin), *"Santa María del Camino"* (Juan Espinosa), *"Santa María de la Esperanza"* (Rafael de Andrés/Juan Espinosa), *"Profetiza Pueblo Mío"* (Rosa Martha Zárate Macías), and *"Grita Profeta"* (Emilio Vicente Matéu)—all popular titles, (sourced from OCP's *Flor y Canto I & II)* won the favor of many. During group gatherings, prayer services and eucharistic celebrations, they became the songs of the assembly. These vernacular hymns of the 1970s embodied the spirit of *Encuentro* and were included in the collection of songs used during the third *Encuentro*.

The spirit of these songs does not apply to a single generation, and each proclaims a permanent message to the Church, defining the pastoral guidelines – a people called to be evangelizers, missionaries, and lovers of justice. They have been included in Hispanic hymnals published in the United States and Spanish-speaking countries and are also included in the Lutheran and Presbyterian English-language hymnals. Thirty years later they are considered part of the common repertoire.[45]

This chapter is but a brief overview of observations from a non-Hispanic writer who has had the privilege and joy of being involved in music ministry with the Hispanic community since high school days. It falls to other writers from within the community to tell the complete story. Catholic music of the 1970s was enriched because of the blessings and gifts shared by this vital and inspiring community of faith.

---

[1] Pérez, Arturo J., "The History of Hispanic Liturgy since 1965," from Dolan, J.P. and Deck, S.J., Allan Figueroa, editors, *Hispanic Catholic Culture in the U.S.: Issues and Concerns,* (University of Notre Dame Press, 1994) 381-382.

[2] Reza, Mary Frances, "Prophetic Voices: Encuentro III," from Colombari, Bari and Prendergast, Michael R., editors, *The Song of the Assembly: Pastoral Music in Practice,* (Portland, Oregon, Pastoral Press, 2007) 42.

[3] *Flor y Canto,* (Portland, Oregon, OCP Publications, 1989), Introduction.

[4] The Servicemen's Readjustment Act of 1944, also known as the G.I. Bill, was a law that provided a range of benefits for returning World War II veterans (commonly referred to as G.I.s). It was designed by the American Legion, who helped push it through Congress by mobilizing its chapters (along with the Veterans of Foreign Wars); the goal was to provide immediate rewards and support for practically all World War II veterans.

[5] This story is true but the names of the priests and the parish are kept anonymous out of respect for the deceased and for the parishioners involved.

[6] Matovina, Timothy, *Latino Catholicism: Transformation in America's Largest Church,* (New Jersey: Princeton University Press, 2012) vii.

[7] Gómez, Raúl R., "Beyond Serapes and Maracas: Liturgical Theology in a Hispanic/Latino Context," *Journal of Hispanic/Latino Theology,* Vol. 8, No. 2, November 2000 (62).

[8] *Lumen Gentium* 11.

[9] Pérez, Arturo J., "The History of Hispanic Liturgy since 1965," from Dolan, J.P. and Deck, S.J., Allan Figueroa, editors, Hispanic Catholic Culture in the U.S.: Issues and Concerns, (University of Notre Dame Press, 1994) 365.

[10] Gómez, 68.

[11] Part of the customary ritual is that every night the couple is rejected, but then accepted at the end of the ritual nightly. The ninth evening it is the same, however since it is *"Noche Buena"* (Christmas Eve) there is a more immediate correlation with the liturgical celebration that leads to the *"acostada del niño."*

[12] Matovina, Timothy, "U.S. Hispanic Catholics and Liturgical Reform," *America,* Vol. 169, November 6, 1993 (18-19).

[13] Matovina, Timothy, *Latino Catholicism: Transformation in America's Largest Church,* (New Jersey: Princeton University Press, 2012) 184.

[14] Simonson, Sharon, "Deconstructing Dia de Los Muertos," *Silicon Valley One World,* October 28, 2015.

[15] Matovina, Timothy, *Latino Catholicism,* 174-175.

[16] Sosa, Juan J., *One Voice, Many Rhythms,* (Portland, Oregon, Pastoral Press, 2008) 63.

[17] Sosa, Juan J., "The Hispanic Presence: Challenge and Commitment," from Colombari, Bari and Prendergast, Michael R., editors, *The Song of the Assembly: Pastoral Music in Practice,* (Portland, Oregon, Pastoral Press, 2007) 38.

[18] Interview with the author, January 29, 2016 in Albuquerque, New Mexico.

[19] Pérez, Arturo J., "The History of Hispanic Liturgy since 1965," from Dolan, J.P. and Deck, S.J., Allan Figueroa, editors, *Hispanic Catholic Culture in the U.S.: Issues and Concerns,* (University of Notre Dame Press, 1994) 384.

[20] Interview with the author, May 10, 2013 in Portland, Oregon.

[21] Pérez, 382.

[22] Interview with the author, January 29, 2016 in Albuquerque, New Mexico.

[23] Interview with the author, May 10, 2013 in Portland, Oregon. The Spanish version of Repp's song is now published by OCP as "Entre Tus Manos."

[24] Pérez, 385.

[25] Interview with the author, January 29, 2016 in Albuquerque, New Mexico.

[26] Moisés Sandoval, ed., *Fronteras* (San Antonio: Mexican American Cultural Center, 1983) 197. As cited in Pérez, 383-384.

[27] Pérez, 384.

[28] *Las Vegas Optic,* September 15, 2011.
http://www.lasvegasoptic.com/content/nuestra-historia-montezuma's-seminary-exile

[29] Interview with the author, November 20, 2017, via email from Albuquerque, New Mexico.

[30] Ibid.

[31] Badillo, David A., "Latino/Hispanic History since 1965: The Collective Transformation of Regional Minorities," from Dolan, J.P. and Deck, S.J., Allan Figueroa, editors, *Hispanic Catholic Culture in the U.S.: Issues and Concerns,* (University of Notre Dame Press, 1994) 54.

[32] Pérez, 386.

[33] Pérez, 387.

[34] Pérez, 389.

[35] For a more complete overview of the early publication history of the Hispanic repertoire, see Pérez, Arturo J., "The History of Hispanic Liturgy since 1965," from Dolan, J.P. and Deck, S.J., Allan Figueroa, editors, *Hispanic Catholic Culture in the U.S.: Issues and Concerns,* (University of Notre Dame Press, 1994) 389-393.

[36] Ibid., 392.

[37] Ridge, M.D., "The Making of Flor y Canto," *Liturgia y Canción,* (Portland, Oregon: OCP Publications, September-November 1997) 5-19.

[38] The Southwest Liturgical Conference (SWLC), founded in 1962, is a liturgical organization comprising the 28 Roman Catholic dioceses of Region X and Region XIII of the Federation of Diocesan Liturgical Commissions (FDLC) in the states of Arizona, Arkansas, Colorado, New Mexico, Oklahoma, Texas, Utah and Wyoming. The SWLC reflects the rich Catholic heritage of the Southwest present in richly diverse multicultural, urban, and rural communities. Working in collaboration with the bishops, diocesan directors of worship and liturgical leaders of the regions served, SWLC provides opportunities for education, formation and networking. See Southwest Liturgical Conference website: www.swlc.org

[39] Interview with the author, January 29, 2016 in Albuquerque, New Mexico.

[40] The word *"encuentro"* is literally translated into English as "encounter."

[41] See USCCB website: http://www.usccb.org/about/public-affairs/backgrounders/national-encuentro.cfm

[42] Interview with the author, May 10, 2013 in Portland, Oregon.

[43] The *Instituto Nacional Hispano de Liturgia* (National Hispanic Institute for Liturgy), is an example of a pastoral institute inspired by *Encuentro.* Formed in the early 1980s, it was influential in the liturgical music that was being developed at the time due to its mandate to assist the U.S. bishops in studying, developing, and promoting the liturgical and spiritual life of Hispanic communities in the United States. This organization, made up of liturgists and liturgical musicians, was at the forefront of planning the liturgies and accompanying the liturgical and prayer life of the many national Hispanic gatherings, including the national *Encuentros* and *Raíces y Alas.* Among the current board members are well-known composers Fr. Juan Sosa, Mary Frances Reza, Rogelio Zelada, Damaris Thillet and Pedro Rubalcava.

[44] See http://www.usccb.org/issues-and-action/cultural-diversity/hispanic-latino/resources/encuentro-in-united-states-hispanic-ministry.cfm

[45] Reza, Mary Frances, "Prophetic Voices: *Encuentro* III," from Colombari, Bari and Prendergast, Michael R., editors, *The Song of the Assembly: Pastoral Music in Practice,* (Portland, Oregon, Pastoral Press, 2007) 41-42.

Musicianship: Challenge and Growth

In the early 1990s, Arturo Pérez made these observations about musicianship and the Hispanic liturgical repertoire.

> Another facet that influenced the religious music market was the lack of trained musicians within the Hispanic community. It is commonly known that many, if not most, Hispanic musicians play and sing by ear rather than by reading music. Few are trained in what constitutes liturgical music, and so they remain very susceptible to selecting music that is well known, can be easily learned, or is suggested by clergy and the community. Only recently has new material been published. Yet, it must be noted that the importation of music, especially from Spain, still outweighs the composition of music and the publication of liturgical resources by local Hispanic composers and authors. The practice of photocopying music, where it still exists, bypasses not only copyright laws, but also jeopardizes the livelihood of the few struggling Hispanic composers and authors who can devote full time to this work. Music publishing companies cannot foster new local music and talent unless there is a balanced economic gain for their encouragement and investment.[1]

In the years since Pérez wrote these words, the situation has improved considerably among Hispanic music ministers, but there are certain unique factors to keep in mind. First, while it is true that many Hispanic musicians play by ear and do not read music, it is important for publishers to print complete notated arrangements: first, for choir directors who rely on standard notation to lead their groups; and second, to inspire ensemble musicians to learn how to read music. Notated sheet music ensures that all singers and musicians are literally on the same page when it comes to interpreting a song at liturgy.

People who are not of Hispanic heritage might not be aware that there are many different styles and rhythms, and many approaches to the music. "The richness and diversity in Latin American countries is unique," Rudy López, Hispanic Events Specialist for OCP explains:

> The United States is a melting pot, so to speak, of so many different cultures from around the world. When you talk about just the Latin American nations, that alone is rich and diverse. For example, we have music from Mexico, Cuba, Puerto Rico, the Dominican Republic, Guatemala, and El Salvador. Each group has its own musical identity. The musical traditions and rhythms of the indigenous people mix with the European approach, and creates a unique blend of sounds. And when those sounds migrate to the United States, another layer of texture is created.[2]

All of these styles are included in songbooks published by OCP, World Library, and other publishers.

To assist musicians in performing these various styles, an elaborate glossary is included in *Flor y Canto II.* Thirty rhythms and styles are identified and notated in brief demonstration measures, including Balada, Blues/Swing, Bolero Cubana, Carnavalito, Habanera, Pambiche, Salsa, Tango, and more.

But these are still sheet music presentations for people who might not be skilled music readers. Recordings are, therefore, indispensable tools for learning new songs and styles, but even more effective are opportunities that allow musicians to meet composers and clinicians and get first-hand demonstrations on performance technique. For more than 15 years, publishers have taken the music to the musicians through local workshops led by a host of respected Hispanic composers, whose numbers have risen dramatically in recent years.

"We're trying to help people discern their calling as musicians, to grow as musicians," said López. "We teach technique, how to read music, how to play the guitar, and how to be a better singer. We give them liturgical formation. And we teach them the songs."[3]

---

[1] Pérez, Arturo J., "The History of Hispanic Liturgy since 1965," from Dolan, J.P. and Deck, S.J., Allan Figueroa, editors, *Hispanic Catholic Culture in the U.S.: Issues and Concerns,* (University of Notre Dame Press, 1994) 390.

[2] Interview with the author, October 11, 2017 in Portland, Oregon.

[3] Ibid.

Chapter Eight

"Come Back to Me with All Your Heart"
The Monks of Weston Priory

In the sacrament of Penance the faithful "obtain from the mercy of God pardon for their sins against him; at the same time, they are reconciled with the Church which they wounded by their sins and which works for their conversion by charity, example and prayer."
                                       -Introduction to the new *Rite of Penance*,
                                              quoting *Lumen Gentium* (no. 11)[1]

You are not forgiven because you confess your sin. You confess your sin, recognize yourself for what you are, *because* you are forgiven.
                                           -Father Herbert McCabe, OP[2]

The vernacular Mass and the allowance of folk music was not the only liturgical change brought about by the Second Vatican Council. For centuries, the Sacrament of Penance was administered within the secure confines of a dark box or "confessional," in which a penitent knelt before a screen that effectively concealed the penitent's identity. The whole experience was often intimidating, especially for young children. But in 1974 the Congregation for Divine Worship approved the new Rite of Penance. Thoughtful pastors immediately commissioned a redesign of their church confessionals that typically created a more open space where priest and penitent could have their "face-to-face" confession. The other wall remained with screen intact so people could have the option for private confession. For some the change was drastic and unwelcome, and news of the changes was not always effectively communicated, leading to comical exchanges where a penitent would walk into a redesigned confessional, startled by a smiling priest who obviously recognized him or her. That sometimes led to a quick dash out the door and to the neighboring parish for a more anonymous confession!

> Under the new liturgy, parishes would be encouraged to hold regular "penitential celebrations" that could be attended by anywhere from a handful to hundreds of people. Individuals will have the opportunity to confess their sins privately to a priest. Absolution will still be granted on an individual basis only.[4]

An Advent or Lent reconciliation service typically consisted of a gathering song, readings from Scripture, a homily by the parish priest, a ritualized examination of conscience, and individual confession. The service concluded with the sign of peace and a song of thanksgiving.

The heart of a reconciliation service, of course, was individual confession, and priests were spread out across the sanctuary, into the sacristy, and into the confessionals. Pastors asked their people to confess only their most troubling transgressions during this service, encouraging them to return on Saturday if they had need of a deeper reconciliation dialogue. Naturally, with a church full of penitents, the period of individual confession could last for more than half an hour, even with several priests serving as confessors.

Parish music groups were often hard pressed to find enough music for the time of individual confessions. The emerging 1970s repertoire provided "Be Not Afraid" and "Turn to Me" by the St. Louis Jesuits. The Monks of Weston Priory were beginning to have an impact, and Gregory Norbet's "Hosea" and "Come to Me" became reconciliation favorites. But music groups needed more songs, and they sometimes reached into the 1960s repertoire by singing Ray Repp's "I Lift Up My Eyes," and Sebastian Temple's "Make Me a Channel of Your Peace." Some music groups even sang secular songs. Liturgical purists cringed, but many parishioners found solace in reflecting on familiar contemporary songs as they waited in the long lines for confession.

As the decades unfolded, participation in the Sacrament of Reconciliation declined. "The statistics are alarming. According to the Center for Applied Research on the Apostolate, a survey in 2005 showed that 42 percent of Catholic adults, when asked how often they went to confession, answered 'Never.'"[5]

This picture might not be as bleak as painted. For every empty church on a Saturday afternoon, there are other parishes that are blessed with compassionate priests who are skilled in the ministry of being a good confessor. Advent and Lent reconciliation services in the 21st century might not draw the overflowing crowds of the 1970s, but there is enough participation there to offer hope for the future.

The Sacrament of Reconciliation has long been an important tool in the search for self, and the discernment of God's will. It is no surprise that it has always been part of the contemplative spirituality of classic monasticism. One monastic community in particular captured the hearts of Catholics and non-Catholics alike through its welcome spirit and gentle music.

Monks of Weston Priory

Weston Priory was founded in 1953 by Abbot Leo Rudloff, a German-born monk who served as the Abbot of Dormition Abbey in Jerusalem. He settled his new Benedictine community in Rutland on an old dairy farm at the edge of the Green Mountain National Forest in Vermont. According to their website, the community's mission is "to live the Gospel of Jesus Christ together. Seeking to be, in Brother Leo's words, 'an embassy of the Reign of God,' we hope that we will, in some measure, foster the healing and reconciliation of the whole human family."[6]

In 2003, their 50th anniversary, they had a community of 15 monks ranging in age between 31 and 81 years old. They gather together five times a day to pray the Liturgy of the Hours and celebrate the Eucharist, and they observe strict silence from the end of Evening Prayer until they pray Morning Prayer.

Although their community is small, the monks of Weston welcome all seekers, men and women, to join them in prayer and solitude.

> Visitors come to Weston Priory for a variety of reasons, ranging from a simple desire to sing with the monks to the deepest kind of longing. While the brothers extend their hospitality to all, they also make it clear that they are unable to provide one-on-one spiritual guidance. For one reason, they are very busy. Between their meals, their prayers and their welcome of a near-constant stream of guests, they run a farm. While visitors are not required to work, they are welcome to.[7]

John Rood of Boston was discerning a possible vocation as a monk at Weston in the early 1970's. He has these memories of his "observership."

> Our daily schedule closely followed what the monks lived. Each day began with a 5:00 a.m. contemplative communal vigil prayer. This was followed by time for personal meditation and spiritual reading, and then an informal pick-up breakfast. Our morning continued with work around the monastery grounds, followed by a celebration of the Eucharist. Next was a substantial midday meal that started out in communal silence with proclaimed spiritual reading, and then some informal conversation. Kitchen chores were followed by a short nap, and then we'd gather in the chapel for Midday Prayer. We then returned to our work, followed by some private time, and then Vespers and a light supper of soup and salad. Recreation was followed by Compline and an early bedtime because of the 5:00 a.m. Vigil Prayer in the morning.

> Work consisted of harvesting forest wood for heating, making repairs and improvements to the physical plant, helping in the office and gift shop, and handling the shipping operation for the many orders of their recordings, songbooks and artwork. We also did daily maintenance and custodial work at the several retreat guesthouses, and we accompanied the monks when needed on shopping trips and errands in town.[8]

The brothers make a living through pottery, weaving, woodwork, calligraphy, and other artistic crafts. But these monks of Weston have something truly unique in comparison with the fudge or honey offered by other religious orders. They share with the world some of the most beloved contemporary Catholic music of the post-Vatican II era.

Born in 1940, Gregory Norbet came from a musical family, singing in his parish choir as a teenager. He took piano lessons, but much to the dismay of his teacher, young Gregory was not performing the actual notes of the printed sheet music, but was playing by ear—even something as complex as Rachmaninoff.

"When television became more common, I inherited the family short wave radio," Gregory recalls:

I had it up in my bedroom and at night. I would hook up a wire to the copper screen, and listen to classical music from all over the world. That's how I learned to arrange. I learned the sense of structure and content, of movement and melody and subtlety. I'm very grateful for that experience because, as my life unfolded, I never had time to study music formally in college or graduate school.

Gregory was a student at Saint Michael's College in Vermont when a friend invited him to Weston Priory to attend Vespers. He was impressed with the poor and humble community of 10 monks. He went back to visit often, and was drawn to the monastic lifestyle. The monks invited him to a retreat, and he discerned a call, joining the Weston Benedictines in 1962.

Weston's founder, Abbot Leo, worked in a pre-Council commission to encourage a more open ecumenical spirit. With the confidence of Pope John XXIII, this commission drafted the Vatican II document *Nostra Aetate* on Christian relations with Jews. Brother Gregory and his fellow monks were basking in the glow of Conciliar optimism, as shared with them by their very own founder.

After the promulgation of the English liturgy in 1964, Brother Gregory knew that because of his community's daily liturgical celebrations, there was a need for new music in the innovative spirit of Vatican II. He was aware of the lively songs of Ray Repp, Sebastian Temple, and others, but that style was not conducive to the contemplative spirit at Weston.

"I started to write during the Council," Norbet remembers:

> and I also was involved with a small group of Benedictine choir directors who were trying to share their adaptations of Gregorian chant from Latin to English. I think most us felt at the time that it wasn't giving us new life, so I composed several anthems because we were singing the Divine Office[9] prior to music being allowed at the vernacular liturgy.

> One night after dinner, before Compline (night prayer), I went up to a room that just had a bare table and a chair and nothing else. It was half of a bedroom cell and I heard in my head a piece of music with the words, 'Peace, I leave with you.' And that was like taking the cork out of the wine bottle. The songs just never stopped after that.[10]

The songs of Brother Gregory were sung in what came to be known as the "Weston Priory sound"—a mesmerizing blend of the chant-like vocals of the brother monks accompanied by gentle guitar. This was simply the music of the monks that attracted hundreds of visitors from around the region.

> Gregorian chant is very powerful, beautiful, high art, and we sang it every day," says Gregory. "I had to write for one or two guitars, and for singers who only knew how to chant in unison. We couldn't sing in harmonies at all. The spirit and sound of my music comes from our grounding in the reflective, contemplative life.[11]

Patrick Berg, a former resident of Rutland, has fond memories of those times.

> My wife and children and I lived about 45 miles away from Weston Priory. We visited on Sundays for liturgy as often as we could. This was between 1974 and 1979; only five years, but they were the years of their most creative musical and liturgical revival. A friend gave me a recording the monks had made. I loved it, and so we went to visit and experience their liturgies ourselves.

> They had a small chapel that was fine for the monks themselves, but because of all the visitors they needed a larger space. They took a barn with huge sliding doors and moved it to the chapel, then moved the altar to the edge of the barn structure so all the people who were visiting could be a part of it. The monks sat in a ring around the altar and we faced them from the barn.[12]

From 300 to 500 people were attending Sunday liturgy at Weston Priory during the warmer months between Easter and November. Brother Gregory printed out his new songs—lyrics and notation—and distributed them to the assembly so they could participate in the singing. Afterward, "Brother Gregory did this post-liturgy workshop where he would get feedback from people," Berg remembers. "He would ask questions. 'How do you like this music? Does it relate to you and your life situation?' It was wonderful because he got people interested and involved."[13]

Naturally, with the increasing awareness of the music of Weston Priory, requests came from visitors to bring that music home in both recorded and printed form. Gregory's friend John Quinn brought recording equipment to the priory and recorded some basic tracks: the monks sang the refrains while Gregory played guitar and sang the verses. Gregory listened to the tracks, and created arrangements for recorder, violin, cello, oboe, and other instruments. Gregory then went to C.I. Recording, his friend's studio in New York, and they had access to some of the finest session musicians in the city.

"There was a wonderful man, Sidney Weinberg, who played oboe for several pieces. At one session I had a chat with him. 'I hope you don't mind my saying this, but I'm looking for the sound of the oboe on Judy Collins' album where she sings 'Send in the Clowns.' And he said, 'That was me.'" [14]

Locusts and Wild Honey, the first album by the Monks of Weston Priory, was released in 1971. Weston's attorney, Norman Bernstein, loved the album, and called his brother Sid Byrnes, the director of ABC News in New York City. "You better get a TV crew up here." The monks and their music were a story on the national news. Without planning or marketing, *Locusts and Wild Honey* took off! The album's liner notes introduced the spirit of Weston's music to scores of new listeners.

> One day our Brother Gregory tried his hand at writing a few melodies for special community celebrations. The results sounded "right" – in the sense that they came out of our own experience, and "natural" as our own surroundings here in the hills of Vermont.[15]

The publication of their sheet music and songbooks is another story altogether. The monks submitted their music to Omer Westendorf at World Library, but this coincided with that company's bankruptcy and acquisition by J.S. Paluch. When the monks did not hear back from Westendorf, they decided to self-publish. All they had was a gift shop and a mailing list—and excellent songs. The sales of their records and songbooks enabled the priory to expand their chapel, and build new retreat quarters for the hundreds of men and women who were now visiting from around the world, drawn by the monks' enchanting songs, the opportunity to pray with them, discern God's will, and find peace.

"I was drawn to Weston by their music," John Rood recalled:

> Their liturgy embodied a real simplicity that seemed to open windows and doors for people. They had a way of making visitors of all faiths—or no faith—feel welcomed and respected. Brother Gregory's songs seemed to emanate from this wholeness.[16]

Gregory Norbet recorded 12 albums with Weston Priory that included iconic songs that are still sung at liturgy today through their inclusion in popular missals and hymnals: "Come to Me," "All I Ask of You," "Wherever You Go," and the amazing "Hosea," a song that often elicits a strong emotional connection. Based on the Old Testament prophet's plea to his unfaithful wife for repentance and reconciliation, the composer painted in broad poetic brushstrokes with lyrics based on key passages from across the prophet's writings.

> Come back to me with all your heart.
> Don't let fear keep us apart.
> Trees do bend, though straight and tall;
> so must we to others' call.
>
> Long have I waited for your coming home to me
> and living deeply our new life.

> Text and music © 1972, The Benedictine Foundation of the State of Vermont, Inc.

The Book of Hosea offers a glimpse into the generous heart of God. Gregory Norbet captured that divine tenderness so eloquently by wrapping his evocative lyrics in one of the most haunting melodies of contemporary Catholic hymnody.

"I remember when Brother Gregory first introduced 'Hosea.' We were stunned!" says Patrick Berg. "After liturgy he asked people, 'What do you think? Would you change anything?' We had no feedback. We were basically blown away."[17]

Every album by Weston Priory was consistently identified as a work by "Your Brothers at Weston." Gregory Norbet was modestly acknowledged for "composition, arrangement, guitar and piano," but the entire musical enterprise was a community effort and presented as such. After 21 years as a Benedictine monk, Norbet moved on from the Weston Priory community. He attended graduate school in Chicago at Loyola and the

Institute for Spiritual Leadership. He continues to compose, and he has released several solo albums with OCP. Gregory and his wife, iconographer Kathryn Carrington, established the Hosea Foundation, whose purpose is to foster the experience of God's love and compassion in the world by promoting spiritual development in individuals and church communities. They have traveled widely as lecturers and retreat leaders.

The Monks of Weston Priory have continued their ministry of outreach to the world, getting involved in peace and social justice concerns, housing refugees, and establishing a community in Cuernavaca, Mexico to raise the consciousness of North Americans to the needs of their southern neighbors.

Music remains the heart of Weston Priory's ministry and they now have 20 albums, with music composed by other monks who have followed in the footsteps of Gregory Norbet. The brothers now market their music online, reaching a whole new generation with their call to contemplation.

---

[1] *The Rites of the Catholic Church as Revised by the Second Vatican Ecumenical Council,* "Rite of Penance," (New York: Pueblo Publishing Co., 1976 (344).

[2] Cornwell, John, *The Dark Box: A Secret History of Confession* (New York: Basic Books, 2014) 238.

[3] *The Rites of the Catholic Church as Revised by the Second Vatican Ecumenical Council,* "Rite of Penance," (New York: Pueblo Publishing Co., 1976 (339-340).

[4] Fiske, Edward B., "Vatican Revises Sacrament of Penance," New York Times, February 7, 1974.

[5] Martin, SJ, James, "Bless me, Father," *America,* May 21, 2017.

[6] Weston Priory website: www.westonpriory.org

[7] Good, Jeffrey, "Weston Priory: A Place Apart," *Valley News* (New Hampshire), August 28, 2012.

[8] Interview with the author, September 20, 2017 via email from Boston, Massachusetts.

[9] Liturgy of the Hours.

[10] Interview with the author, November 5, 2015, by phone in West Lebanon, New Hampshire.

[11] Ibid.

[12] Interview with the author, September 12, 2017, in Portland, Oregon.

[13] Ibid.

[14] Interview with the author, November 5, 2015, by phone in West Lebanon, New Hampshire.

[15] Liner notes for *Locusts and Wild Honey,* the first album by the Monks of Weston Priory (1971).

[16] Interview with the author, September 20, 2017 via email from Boston, Massachusetts.

[17] Interview with the author, September 12, 2017, in Portland, Oregon.

Cursillo and Marriage Encounter: Movements in the Church

The 1970s is a decade frequently characterized by its inward focus: the self-esteem movement. The Catholic Church would never admit to any direct association with the movement, but its various secular manifestations certainly influenced such areas as religious education, youth ministry, and liturgical music.

Catholic music critic Thomas Day connects contemporary liturgical music with the self-esteem movement in his polemical book, *Why Catholics Can't Sing:*

> The victory of the folk style, reformed or otherwise, is so great and so blinding that many people cannot see beyond that apparent success to what could mildly be called the *problem* with this music: simply put, nearly all of it—no matter how sincere, no matter how many scriptural texts it contains—oozes with an indecent narcissism. The folk style, as it has developed since the 1960s, is Ego Renewal put to music. . . The music always seems to be assuring everybody that the good news of the New Testament goes something like this: "I'm OK, you're OK, God's OK" – in that order.[1]

This harsh criticism is compelling food for thought. It can be argued that composers of contemporary liturgical music are not consciously wearing the clothes of the self-esteem movement, but simply reflecting how modern Christians express their search for God in the post-Conciliar era. The same criticism can be levied against Bach, Luther, Palestrina and the anonymous composers of Gregorian chant, all of whom were once considered contemporary in their day. The main difference, of course, is that these composers did not have to deal with the influence of self-esteem.

In and of itself, there is nothing wrong with the inward journey, but a Catholic approach helps the seeker to find Christ at the center of that search for self. In the 1970s, this approach was reflected in at least two major Catholic movements.

Cursillo

Cursillos de Cristiandad (Cursillos in Christianity) is a three-day weekend experience that had its origins in Mallorca, Spain in 1944, by a group of laymen who were concerned about training Christian leaders. The movement was led by Eduardo Bonnín Aguiló, an outgoing intellectual who had a deep and abiding passion for helping lay people to develop their spiritual lives.

> Eduardo wanted the culture of the time to change. He wanted people to *want* to change the culture and he wanted people to be great friends. The culture he wanted to change was one marked by authoritarianism, fascist rhetoric and violence, and a deep sense of mistrust among Mallorquines. Bonnín encouraged *amistad* (friendship) and wanted people to get along and accept their differences.[2]

Bonnín developed the idea of "short courses" (hence, the Spanish name *"cursillos"*) over a three-day weekend, with several talks *("rollos")* given by lay people and priests on the basics of the Catholic faith. Each talk is followed by discussion in designated small groups. Over the years, the weekend came to include the celebration of the Eucharist, an opportunity for the Sacrament of Penance, adoration before the Blessed Sacrament, fellowship, shared meals, and group singing. Friends and family members offer their prayerful support *("palancas")* during the weekend. The goal of Cursillo is to inspire participants to take what they have learned back into the world during their "fourth day," that is, the rest of their lives. This fourth day is supported by regular group reunions *("ultreyas")* in their home communities with fellow participants known as *"cursillistas." Cursillos de Cristiandad* began as a men's movement, but weekends for women began in 1953.

The Cursillo movement came to North America in 1957 when the first weekend was held in Waco, Texas. All weekends were held in Spanish until 1961, when the first English-speaking weekend was held in San Angelo, Texas. From there, the movement exploded into popularity across the United States and around the world.

"Cursillo was crucial," said Mary Frances Reza. "My husband and I were both active in the Cursillo movement. Henry was a rector for many of the Cursillos, and I was a *profesora.* The Cursillo movement had a large impact on our Hispanic community. After the Cursillo movement, came the Charismatic Renewal."[3]

In San Francisco, during the height of the Second Vatican Council (1962-65), Cursillo weekends started welcoming Episcopalians as leaders and participants. Not surprisingly, after Protestants got a taste of Cursillo, many leaders wanted to bring that experience to their own denominations, but with a less Catholic slant. Such offshoots include Tres Dias (Reform tradition), Via de Cristo (Lutheran), Walk to Emmaus (Methodist), and Kairos Prison Ministry International (Cursillo experience for incarcerated men and women and their families). All maintain denominational roots but simultaneously emphasize an ecumenical spirit.

> Since the late 1950s, millions of American Catholics and Protestants and Christians around the world have participated in a 72-hour Cursillo weekend course, or one of its many spinoffs. Catholic and Protestant graduates of the weekend Cursillo claim to be new individuals, refreshed and renewed. Cursillistas seek to demonstrate their new identities by living a life they believe Christ would want them to live.[4]

"So many of the *cursillista* men became deacons," Mary Frances Reza remembered. "Leadership roles changed. What I loved about the Cursillo movement was the way it taught the *cursillistas* to look for their leaders. If you're teaching, if you're working, wherever you are, look for the leaders. Focus on developing their leadership. These are the people you call to Cursillo."[5]

Marriage Encounter

Marriage Encounter is a predominantly Roman Catholic movement whose goal is to teach married couples how to communicate more effectively. It began in 1962 when Father Gabriel Calvo developed a series of conferences for couples to develop an open and honest relationship and live out their sacramental marriage in the service of others. Beginning in Barcelona, the weekend conferences became very successful and spread rapidly through Spain.

In 1966, Father Calvo and a married couple addressed the International Confederation of Christian Family Movements in Caracas, Venezuela. From there, the weekend program spread through Latin America and to Spanish speaking couples in the United States.

In 1967, a couple and a priest presented the weekend experience in English to seven couples and a few priests at the Christian Family Movement convention at Notre Dame University. By 1968, 50 couples and 29 priests were presenting weekends throughout the United States.

In 1969, a national executive board was formed to coordinate the fast-growing movement in the United States and Canada. Father Chuck Gallagher and several couples in the New York area began to develop their own variation on the weekend experience by emphasizing the importance of follow-up to the actual weekend experience and the development of a Marriage Encounter community so couples could support each other after their initial weekend. Philosophical differences led to a separation of the National Marriage Encounter movement and Father Gallagher's approach, which became known as Worldwide Marriage Encounter. Both groups exist today as two different expressions of the original experience developed by the founder, Father Calvo.[6]

What is the Marriage Encounter method?

> At the retreats, couples are taught a communication technique called the "10 and 10." After being assigned a topic by a clergyman, each couple writes down their deepest feelings about a subject for 10 minutes, then they discuss their written comments for another 10 minutes. The subjects include how the couples met, what they would like to be doing in 10 years, and how they feel about being parents. At the retreats, a couple does this in the privacy of their room. The goal is to encourage the couples to write each other a letter every day expressing their feeling on a topic they select.[7]

Over the years, encountered couples have attested to the positive difference Marriage Encounter has made for their lifelong commitment. Of course, there are always detractors to any movement. Many couples who have attended encounter weekends have felt the dialogue techniques were tedious and too much of a ritual. Those who tried to continue the letter writing practice at home found it to be too repetitive.

Marriage Encounter received the Pope's blessing. At a 1986 conference in Tampa, Florida, Archbishop Pio Laghi, at the time Papal Nuncio to the United States, shared this message from Pope John Paul II:

> "I convey to you the blessing of the Holy Father," he said to those in the festive crowd who linked hands during the singing of the Lord's Prayer. He read them a four-page letter from Pope John Paul II congratulating Worldwide Marriage Encounter for its efforts "to inspire married couples with a true Christian vision of their vocation to marriage and family life."[8]

Exact statistics are difficult to track for a grassroots organization but a *New York Times* article from 1986 gives an indication of the growth of Marriage Encounter during its heyday.

> Estimates of the number of couples who have participated in all such programs run into the millions, but so informal are many organizations that no accurate tally exists. Worldwide Marriage Encounter estimates that 1.5 million people have participated in its own encounter weekends.[9]

Today, Marriage Encounter is a truly worldwide ecumenical movement. The experience is recommended by many dioceses in the United States as one of many options to promote healthy and loving marriages. "As of 2015, the Weekend is now offered in numerous languages and dialects in nearly 100 countries." [10]

How do these spiritual movements affect and influence the life of the Church? The Diocese of Brooklyn conducted a study on this question and the results were very revealing.

> Perhaps the most important finding was that spiritual movements like Charismatic Renewal, Cursillo and Marriage Encounter have produced many of the most loyal and active parish members, rather than leading spiritually minded Catholics out of parish life.[11]

One way of understanding the Catholic movements of the 1970s is to contrast them with the parish societies that were so prevalent in the 1940s and 50s, such as the Holy Name Society and the Women's Guild. Those groups were under the direct supervision of their pastor, who made sure to nurture their spirituality. But such societies were often geared toward the physical services they could provide to the parish plant: painting the school, cleaning the altar and vestments, and other such tasks.

In contrast, Cursillo, Marriage Encounter, and charismatic prayer groups of the 1970s were not under the direct supervision of the pastor and were generally not concerned with the health of the physical plant of the parish, but rather the spiritual health of its members.

1   Day, Thomas, *Why Catholics Can't Sing* (New York: Crossroad, 1990) 60, 64.

2   Nabhan-Warren, Kristy, *The Cursillo Movement in America: Catholics, Protestants, and Fourth-Day Spirituality.* (Chapel Hill: The University of North Carolina Press, 2013) 21.

3   Interview with the author, January 30, 2016 from Albuquerque, New Mexico.

4   Nabhan-Warner, 2.

5   Interview with the author, January 30, 2016 from Albuquerque, New Mexico.

6   See Worldwide Marriage Encounter website: www.wwme.org

7   Johnson, Sharon, "Marriage Boosters Hold a Conference on the Coast," *New York Times*, August 12, 1980.

8   Collins, Glenn, "The Family! 1,700 Couples Meet to Improve Marriages," *New York Times*, July 21, 1986.

9   Ibid.

10 See Worldwide Marriage Encounter website: www.wwme.org

11 Vecsey, George, "Catholics Reassess Views on Spiritual Movements," *New York Times*, July 16, 1978. Brooklyn officials are quick to point out that their study indicates trends unique to the ethnic make-up of their diocese and should not be applied in a blanket way to the entire US church.

Chapter Nine

"We Hold a Treasure"
The National Association of Pastoral Musicians

We go where words cannot go. We shape the spirituality of our people through our music.

-Elaine Rendler[1]

The entire worshipping assembly exercises a ministry of music. Some members of the community, however, are recognized for the special gifts they exhibit in leading the music, praise, and thanksgiving of Christian assemblies. These are the pastoral musicians, whose ministry is especially cherished by the Church.

-*Liturgical Music Today,* **No. 63**[2]

If they sing it in the shower, they'll sing it well in church.

-Eugene Walsh, S.S.[3]

Father Virgil Funk had a vision that put him in deep financial trouble. The National Association of Pastoral Musicians (NPM) that he helped found in 1976 was already in debt by $64,000. Less than a year later, he was drafting a letter to the Association's 2,100 parish-affiliated members to announce bankruptcy. The young, dark-haired priest looked out across his modest office in the basement of Saint Mark Parish in Hyattsville, Maryland. His dedicated staff included Sister Jane Marie Perrot, DC, former executive secretary of the National Catholic Music Educators Association, now working as music consultant, advertising manager, and circulation manager of *Pastoral Music;* Bill Detweiler, Episcopal priest and magazine editor, and Gerry Valerio, who did layout and design; Father Bill Saulnier, executive director, who was primarily responsible for membership and promotion; and NPM's secretary Kay Meyers who worked with Funk on a campaign to solicit new members. This staff was either working without pay or on the promise of future pay.

Father Virgil left a secure position as executive director of the long-established Liturgical Conference when his proposal of focusing on musicians was voted down by the conference's national staff. He decided to start a separate organization based upon the returns of a questionnaire he sent to 3,000 musicians and clergy. He would move forward if he received 60 positive responses; he received only 48, but charged ahead anyway.

"We decided to focus on the *people* who would lead the renewal and need renewal themselves," said Funk:

That is why we chose the name Pastoral *Musicians* and not Pastoral *Music* for the association, though we kept the second title for our magazine. Repertoire, while important, is not the solution to the problems that we face. Our focus was—and is—on the musician: Good musicians make good music.

To promote this ideal, the association initially offered only one form of membership: clergy and musician together from the same parish.[4]

There were some encouraging signs. Bishop Joseph Hodges of Wheeling-Charleston, West Virginia, sent a donation of $1,000 to support what he referred to as the association's "good cause." Sandra Kalenick, a professional promotion copy writer, was also impressed with Virgil's vision and wrote an outstanding promotional letter. But promotional letters are only as good as the people who receive them, and the larger the pool of recipients, the better.

That large pool was provided by Robert Batastini, general editor of Catholic music publisher GIA, which had a strict rule of never renting or selling its mailing list of 20,000 church musicians. But Batastini also believed in Virgil Funk's vision of an association of musicians and, with the approval of GIA President Ed Harris, that valuable mailing list was shared with NPM.

And then there was the enthusiasm of Father Tom Banick from the Office of Liturgy in Scranton, Pennsylvania. He called Virgil to share an idea that would prove to be a game changer. "We need to have a convention, some sort of gathering to bring the musicians together."

"I could sense his excitement about this idea," Funk recalled, "and I was getting excited about it as well. But I had to tell him the truth of our financial situation and our staffing problems."

Father Banick was undeterred. "Let's do it in Scranton. You get the speakers and we will staff it." Within days, Banick secured Marywood College as a venue and lined up volunteers to help get the convention off the ground.

"We went to Scranton because Father Tom Banick and his team of volunteers believed so strongly in what we were doing," Funk said. "So, at our darkest moment, in debt to our ears, hanging on to the slender hope that Sandra Kalenick's promotional letter sent to the GIA mailing list would work, we began planning for the First Annual NPM National Convention, scheduled for March, 1978."[5]

Never underestimate the power of great vision!

Virgil Funk was born in 1937 in La Crosse, Wisconsin. His family moved to Arlington, Virginia and he entered Saint Charles Minor Seminary in Baltimore, Maryland, at age 14. While attending Saint Mary's Seminary, also in Baltimore, he developed his love for liturgy, inspired by his mentor, Sulpician Father Eugene Walsh, distinguished liturgist. Funk sang in the seminary choir, which had earned a stellar reputation by singing both traditional chant and contemporary vernacular choral works under

Walsh's direction. He did biblical studies with Sulpician Father Raymond Brown, eminent Scripture scholar, and he sang along with Folk Mass composer Joe Wise, who was also a student at Saint Mary's. Funk graduated with advanced degrees in sacred theology and sacred Scripture and was ordained a priest for the Diocese of Richmond in 1968.

After ordination, Funk received a master's degree in social work and community organizing. He served as an assistant in the Richmond Catholic Family and Children's Services, a diocesan-wide ministry that addressed family needs, adoption services, and the placement of at-risk children.

When it came to the liturgy, people were already asking why the Council wasn't working. Why wasn't the Church being renewed? Funk was appointed as pastor out of seniority sequence—only six years as a priest—specifically to implement the liturgical principles of the Second Vatican Council on the parish level.

As director of music for the Diocese of Richmond, Funk worked tirelessly to assist parishes in the transition to the vernacular liturgy. Amidst all this activity, he found time to teach music and song to the Visitation Sisters living in his parish, working with them to make their daily Mass come alive. This blending of knowledge and experience in social work, community organizing, and liturgy would serve him well in his life's work.

Funk remembers how NPM got started:

> It all began in 1969, when I was diocesan director of music. I had organized a diocesan organ workshop and Connie Beck, a local organist, asked, 'Why don't we Catholics have an organization like the American Guild of Organists,' When I answered that Catholics should join the AGO since it is such a fine organization, she continued, 'but we need something that focuses on the changes that are taking place in Catholic liturgy, not just techniques for organists.' That exchange planted a seed that bore fruit nine years later.[6]

When Funk went to the national level and became the executive director of the Liturgical Conference in 1974, the organization had already weathered the withdrawal of the support of the United States Bishops Conference. With the loss of episcopal sponsorship, the conference responded by becoming an ecumenical organization.

Funk's two years with the Liturgical Conference put him in contact with the finest ecumenical liturgical leadership in the country. He also saw first-hand what was involved in managing a major convention. Now, on March 28, 1978, Funk and his staff were anxiously waiting at Marywood College in Scranton, Pennsylvania, to see if anyone would be coming to the First (hopefully) Annual Pastoral Musicians National Convention.

The official brochure for the first NPM convention was certainly enticing. Keynote speakers included Jesuit Father John Gallen, director of the Notre Dame Center for Pastoral Liturgy ("Musical Liturgy Is On the Way"); Alexander Peloquin, composer-in-residence at Boston College ("A Lively History of Music in Liturgy"); the St. Louis Jesuits ("Relating Music to the Liturgy"); and the Benedictine Father Nathan Mitchell, assistant professor of liturgy and doctrinal theology, Saint Meinrad School of Theology ("The Changing Role of the Pastoral Musician").

Special events included an opportunity to voice concerns; eucharistic liturgy and Liturgy of the Hours offering "the beauty of the Roman Rite like you have never experienced it before;" showcases and exhibits by the leading publishers; and opportunities for do-it-yourself jam sessions: Bring your instruments!

The NPM staff tempered their expectations, hoping for a modest 600 attendees. 1,400 people showed up! The staff had to scramble, and arranged for the major presentations and eucharistic liturgies to be presented twice; but this was surely a good problem to have.

Dan Schutte has this memory of that first convention liturgy:

> The St. Louis Jesuits arrived in Scranton and we were welcomed warmly by Virgil Funk. And he said, 'Guys, I have a big favor to ask of you. 1,400 people will never fit into any of the churches around here. So, we're having three convention liturgies. Would you be willing to lead one of them?'
>
> I will always remember the thrill of hearing those hundreds of voices singing with us, without even teaching them the songs. There weren't enough printed worship aids, but people sang along anyway.[7]

Those 1,400 musicians and priests learned new repertoire, met composers, and opened themselves up to liturgical theology through the insights of nationally recognized speakers. Equally important was the mutual support they found in networking and praying with fellow church musicians. No longer did they feel alone. At that first NPM gathering, lifelong friendships were forged, many of which continue to this day. People couldn't wait for the following year's convention!

"Dolly Sokol was the diocesan director of liturgy in Chicago," said Funk. "She came to me during Scranton and said, 'We have got to do this in Chicago!' The fire was lit." Dr. Elaine Rendler, who has been with NPM since the beginning, has a fond memory of that second convention that clearly demonstrates how NPM uplifted the liturgical imagination of the participants:

> The call to worship for the Chicago convention's eucharistic liturgy—Bernstein's 'Simple Song' from *Mass*, accompanied by a single guitar—was followed immediately with the entrance processional, Bach's 'Jesu, Joy of Man's Desiring.' It was sung SATB by the entire congregation, accompanied by orchestra. The whole seemed greater than the sum of the parts. Some said it was truly the work of the Holy Spirit.[8]

After the next convention city is chosen, how are the theme, speakers and workshops determined?

106

"I'm a felt-need organizer which means I don't want to impose upon you my organization," Funk explained. "What I want to do is find out what *you* need to help you be organized, and I will assist you in that act of organizing. So, I am subordinate to the process.

> A year before each convention, I gathered representatives from the dioceses of the host region. It was a gathering of diocesan directors and musicians from that area, and we met for two days. We started off in the morning with the question, 'What is it that's keeping your community from a more effective celebration of the Eucharist?' I said, 'I don't want you to give me the answer of what's wrong or how to fix it. I want to find out. Until we name the problem, you can't create a solution.' We had chart paper all over the walls of the meeting room, and we identified problems or concerns. We noted problems that were similar.

> That night we created themes of the convention by linking together the problems that were identified. The next morning, we got up and analyzed our dreams. How did last night's ideas sit? Are you excited about this? Is this going to be something that people are going to be enthused about? Did we identify the problems, and are these the people that will help us to deal with them? Is this the theme? After we came to a consensus, we then worked on workshop topics and presenters.

> So, the people who were organizing the convention had ownership. It was *their* convention. The NPM office wasn't coming in and saying, 'We're going to do it this way.'[9]

Over the years, this process led to a remarkable series of convention themes, presented at national and regional conventions.[10] "The themes of the major conventions, when stitched together, provide a touchstone for the major issues of the liturgy," Funk went on to say:

> When we did needs analysis from the church musicians, what they consistently asked for was more liturgical education. We were always surprised that the musicians were aware of their lack of training in the area of the liturgical renewal. That was one of the elements that we felt that the association had to contribute. The National Association of Pastoral Musicians emerged at a time when we needed pastoral music. We needed repertoire desperately.[11]

Hence, NPM conventions became the primary national forum for publishers and composers to present their new music at showcase concerts and breakout sessions. Indeed, one of the major highlights of attending a convention was the opportunity to bring home octavos, songbooks and recordings of new music to try at liturgy back at the parish. But formation before repertoire was the key.

"We attracted to the National Association of Pastoral Musicians the best liturgical academics of our time as speakers," Funk said, and so, we were deliberately cross-feeding the church musicians with as much information as possible about the liturgical movement, and the liturgical rites, as well as the practical way of implementing the renewal of the rites.

The relationship between liturgy and music is a tension that we identified early in NPM. The first expression of it was in the language that we used. For example, the theme of the first convention was 'Musical Liturgy Is Normative.' That means it's normal for music to be part of a liturgy. That was a revolutionary idea because, prior to the Second Vatican Council, the norm was that music was an add-on that took place only at certain times.

Musical liturgy is normative is the foundational idea of the National Association of Pastoral Musicians. Musicians are subordinate to the liturgy and therefore it's not an association of musicians only. It's an association of musicians who are at service to the liturgy.[12]

The last convention with Funk at the helm was in 2001, and had the theme "Musical Liturgy Is Transformative."

"If the music effectively celebrates the liturgy, it will create a transformation in the assembly as well as in the musicians themselves. Those two ideas link together. Transformation and musical liturgy are normative; musical liturgy is transformative," said Funk.

This principle of placing musicians before the music, and musicians at the service the liturgy is at the heart of the new name that Funk created to replace "church musician." Elaine Rendler, editor of *Today's Liturgy* magazine and longtime NPM associate, explained:

Why the name 'pastoral musician'? Father Funk said the inspiration for the name came from the Second Vatican Council, which was not primarily dogmatic but pastoral. For the new organization, it meant identity. For the members, it also meant belonging to something greater than ourselves. We were no longer solitary in our ministry. Our task was unique and we had a name: *pastoral musician.* The name helped clarify who we are and also our unique art form. As pastoral musicians, we are servants of the liturgy, bound by the yoke of liturgical, musical and pastoral praxis as understood currently in *Sing to the Lord* [a USCCB document], which uses the term 'pastoral musician' seven times.[13]

In addition to the annual national conventions, NPM comes home by bringing pastoral musicians together in local chapters that meet regularly for support and prayer. The association has two major divisions: the director of Music Ministries Division and the Music Educators Division. NPM also has standing committees for special interests. NPM members engage in the activity of the association by participating actively in special interest sections. Each section is directed by its own standing committee and provides opportunities for sharing and education.[14]

Virgil Funk retired as president of NPM in 2001 on the association's 25th anniversary. His thick mane of hair has turned a distinctive silver, but he still has that youthful sparkle in his eye that engages people and inspires them to participate. Retiring in Portland, Oregon, he is involved in his local community, supporting his parish pastoral musicians and working for ecumenism by bringing his neighborhood Catholic and Lutheran parishes together for prayer and community service projects. Virgil's vision remains vital and clear.

1   *Pastoral Music,* Vol. 5, No. 5 (June-July 1981), as quoted in *Fostering the Art of Musical Liturgy: 25 Years of Service* (Washington, DC: NPM Publications, 2001) 3.

2   *Liturgical Music Today,* (Washington, DC: United States Catholic Conference) No. 63, as quoted in Joncas, Jan Michael, *From Sacred Song to Ritual Music: Twentieth-Century Understandings of Roman Catholic Worship Music* (Collegeville, MN: The Liturgical Press, 1997) 90.

3   As quoted in Leonard, Timothy, *Geno: A Biography of Eugene Walsh, S.S,* (Washington, DC: Pastoral Press, 1988) 88.

4   *Fostering the Art of Musical Liturgy: 25 Years of Service* (Washington, DC: NPM Publications, 2001) 17.

5   Ibid., 18.

6   Ibid., 15.

7   Interview with the author, September 1, 2014 in San Francisco, California.

8   Rendler, Elaine, "How Firm a Foundation: NPM's Basic Principles," *Pastoral Music* (September 2016), 23.

9   Interview with the author, October 9, 2017, in Portland, Oregon.

10 This list is only a sampling. Until 2002, NPM conventions alternated between national and regional conventions. The regionals offered an opportunity for NPM to reach out to more diverse communities beyond the major cities of the United States.

11 Interview with the author, October 9, 2017, in Portland, Oregon.

12 Ibid.

13 Rendler, Elaine, "How Firm a Foundation: NPM's Basic Principles," *Pastoral Music* (September 2016), 22-23. *Sing to the Lord* is the 2007 document on liturgical music issued by the United States Conference of Catholic Bishops.

14 *Fostering the Art of Musical Liturgy: 25 Years of Service* (Washington, DC: NPM Publications, 2001) 67.

The American Documents on the Liturgy

In the 1970s and 80s, the Bishops Committee for the Liturgy (BCL) issued two documents that guided the celebration of the Eucharist for Catholics in the United States.

Music in Catholic Worship (MCW), issued in 1972, built upon *The Place of Music in Eucharistic Celebrations,* the preliminary liturgy document of 1967, which was notable in the way it defined the "three judgments" for evaluating liturgical music: musical judgment, liturgical judgment, and pastoral judgment.[1]

In his book, *From Sacred Song to Ritual Music,* liturgical theologian and composer Michael Joncas offers a concise overview of the various documents on the liturgy. He gives the following summary of *Music in Catholic Worship:*

> After an introduction noting how the BCL had issued a document on the place of music in Eucharistic celebration in 1967, MCW begins with a theology of liturgical celebrations (1-9). A second segment deals with pastoral planning for liturgical celebration (10-14), specifying that attention must be paid to the congregation (15-18), the occasion (19-20), and the celebrant (21-22). The heart of MCW appears in the next section on the place of music in liturgical celebration.[2]

Appearing in 1982, *Liturgical Music Today (LMT)* was also issued by the BCL as a commentary upon and extension of MCW:

> Since the Roman liturgical books were still in the process of revision ten years ago, the Committee recognizes that there are subjects that *Music in Catholic Worship* addressed only briefly or not at all, such as music within the sacramental rites and in the Liturgy of the Hours. Moreover, the passage of time has raised a number of unforeseen issues in need of clarification and questions revealing new possibilities for liturgical music. We take this opportunity to note these developments. This statement, therefore, should be read as a companion to *Music in Catholic Worship* and *Environment and Art in Catholic Worship* (3).

The stance taken toward Roman Rite worship music in MCW is even more strongly emphasized in *LMT*:

> These guidelines concern the Church's liturgy, which is inherently musical. If music is not valued within the liturgy, then this statement will have little to offer. On the other hand, if music is appreciated as a necessarily normal dimension of every experience of communal worship, then what follows may help to promote continued understanding of the liturgy, dialogue among those responsible for its implementation, and music itself as sung prayer (5).

Joncas noted:

> We see here a progression from *Sacrosanotum Concilium*'s (SC) claim that texted vocal music is a necessary or integral part of the solemn liturgy

through *MCW*'s assertion that, as part of the symbolic character of worship, music should ideally be part of every liturgical celebration to *LMT*'s declaration that the Church's liturgy is 'inherently musical,' a 'necessarily normal dimension of every experience of communal worship.'[3]

Highlighting the permission to mix sung languages in a single celebration given by the Sacred Congregation for Divine Worship's follow-up to *SC, Muscian Sacram, LMT* opts for an eclectic approach to choosing repertoire.

> Different languages may be used in the same celebration. This may also be said of mixing different musical idioms and media. For example, pastoral reasons might suggest that in a given liturgical celebration some music reflect classical hymnody, with other music drawn from gospel or 'folk' idioms, from contemporary service music, or from the plainsong or polyphonic repertoire (14).

> While this principle upholding musical plurality has pastoral value, it should never be employed as a license for including poor music (15).

LMT is notable for its forthright recognition of the multicultural dimensions of Roman Rite worship in many sections of the United States.

> Just as the great liturgical music of the past is to be remembered, cherished and used, so also the rich diversity of the cultural heritage of the many peoples of our country today must be recognized, fostered and celebrated. The United States of America is a nation of nations, a country in which people speak many tongues, live their lives in diverse ways, celebrate events in song and music in the folkways of their cultural, ethnic and racial roots (54).

These are but a few highlights of two important documents that helped give direction to American priests, liturgists, pastoral musicians, composers, and all those who participate in the sacred liturgy. In her preface to a published booklet of the documents, Elaine Rendler noted, "I cannot begin to imagine what it would be like to serve in the ministry of music without the guidance of the two documents. I think I would feel like a navigator without a compass or, worse, up a creek without a paddle."[4]

---

[1] See Canedo, Ken, *Keep the Fire Burning: The Folk Mass Revolution* (Portland, OR: Pastoral Press, 2009) 110.

[2] Joncas, Jan Michael, *From Sacred Song to Ritual Music: Twentieth-Century Understandings of Roman Catholic Worship Music* (Collegeville, MN: The Liturgical Press, 1997) 6.

[3] Ibid., 24.

[4] Bishops' Committee on the Liturgy, *The Music Documents: Music in Catholic Worship and Liturgical Music Today,* (Portland, OR: Oregon Catholic Press, 1995) 4.

Chapter Ten

"I Surrender"
Transitions in the Papacy
and John Michael Talbot

Yesterday morning, I went to the Sistine Chapel to vote peacefully. I never would have imagined what was to take place.[1]
> -Albino Luciani (John Paul I)

The cardinals have called for a new bishop of Rome. They called him from a faraway land—far and yet always close because of our communion in faith and Christian traditions. I was afraid to accept that responsibility, yet I do so in a spirit of obedience to the Lord and total faithfulness to Mary, our most Holy Mother.[2]
> -Karol Wojtyla, on the Vatican balcony
> after his election as Pope John Paul II

Take all my freedom, my liberty, my will.
All that I have, you've given to me.
So I offer it up to you.
> -John Michael Talbot, from his song "I Surrender"

October 4, 1965, was an *extraordinary* day in New York, a city that was perhaps jaded from the overuse of that word by Madison Avenue hype and the local press. On this day, Pope Paul VI, the Vicar of Christ on Earth, set foot on American soil, and in 14 short, but busy hours, captivated the city, the country, and the world. "Who would ever have thought that the Pope of Rome would one day say Mass in Yankee Stadium?"[3] Pope Paul's message to the United Nations was simple, bold, and direct: "Never again war, never again war! It is peace, peace, that has to guide the destiny of the nations of all mankind!"[4]

Giovanni Battista Montini was a man of his times. During his childhood in Brescia, he observed his father, a member of the Italian parliament, and a director of Catholic Action—a lay organization that encouraged Catholic influence on society. Schooled by the Jesuits, young Giovanni was ordained a priest in 1920, and received a doctorate in Canon Law that same year. At age 25, he was invited to serve the Vatican Secretariat of State, and became the papal nuncio to Poland in 1923. A skilled organizer, he would go on to an ecclesial career that included service in the Roman Curia as a close advisor to Pope Pius XII during the tumultuous years of World War II. His work to shelter refugees in convents, parishes, and seminaries drew the ire of Italian dictator Benito Mussolini himself.

In 1954, he was appointed as Archbishop of Milan. As archbishop, he showed an interest in labor issues and working conditions, and engaged in ecumenical and inter-faith dialogue with Protestants and Muslims, and met with atheists. Pope John XXIII elevated Montini as a cardinal in 1958, and he worked behind the scenes to assist in preparations for the Second Vatican Council.

Given his pastoral and administrative background, and his closeness to both Pius XII and John XXIII, Montini's election as pope in 1963 came as no surprise. The new Pope Paul VI immediately went to work to continue the Second Vatican Council begun by his predecessor. When he closed the Council in 1965, he had set into motion an ambitious agenda that centered on liturgical reform, collegiality among the bish-ops, and Christian unity, seeking more open relations with the leadership of Eastern Orthodox and Protestant churches. He famously donated the priceless papal tiara to the Basilica of the National Shrine of the Immaculate Conception in Washington, DC, as a gift to the American people.

As the first pope to travel outside of Italy in more than 150 years, he visited all six inhabited continents, highlighted with journeys to the Holy Land, India, Uganda, and the United Nations. After a 1970 assassination attempt in Manila, the Philip-pines, Pope Paul never again traveled outside of Italy, preferring instead to write encyclicals, preside over synods, and receive diplomats and dignitaries at the Vatican.

Pope Paul's impressive accomplishments are many, but they are perhaps unfairly over-shadowed by the firestorm of reaction to his 1968 encyclical, *Humanae Vitae,* in which he sought to clarify the Catholic Church's teaching on human life and its beginnings.

> Marriage and conjugal love are by their nature ordained toward the procre-ation and education of children. Children are really the supreme gift of mar-riage and contribute in the highest degree to their parents' welfare.

> We base our words on the first principles of a human and Christian doctrine of marriage when we are obliged once more to declare that the direct inter-ruption of the generative process already begun and, above all, all direct abortion, even for therapeutic reasons, are to be absolutely excluded as lawful means of regulating the number of children. Equally to be condemned, as the magisterium of the Church has affirmed on many occasions, is direct sterilization, whether of the man or of the woman, whether permanent or temporary [*Humanae Vitae,* Pope Paul VI].

An editorial from *The National Catholic Review* stated:

> In the final years of his life, Paul VI often spoke of the burdens of age and the imminence of death. Yet these shadows did not paralyze his spirit or cause him to shrink from the challenges of a dangerous world. He condemned the increasing violence of the age and sought repeatedly to strike a responsive chord in the moral conscience of his contemporaries.[5]

Pope Paul VI (1963-1978) reigned over what was arguably the most tumultuous period in Catholic Church history since the Protestant Reformation. As the College of Cardinals arrived in Rome for the funeral and the conclave, there was great speculation in the media on who would succeed this Pilgrim Pope who very deftly led his Church into the modern world.

On August 26, 1978, after the fourth ballot, the College of Cardinals elected Cardinal Albino Luciani, the Patriarch of Venice, as the 263rd successor to Saint Peter. The new pope took on an unprecedented double name to honor his two immediate predecessors: John Paul I.

Albino Luciani was born in Forno di Canale in Belluno, Northern Italy. His father Giovani, a bricklayer, gave his approval when Albino asked permission at age 10 to enter the seminary. He advised his son, "I hope that when you become a priest you will be on the side of the workers, for Christ himself would have been on their side."[6] Albino would be the first pope of modern times to come from a working-class family.

He was ordained in 1935, serving for a short while as a parish priest before accepting a teaching assignment at his own seminary in Belluno, eventually becoming vice-rector. As a professor of dogmatic and moral theology, Father Luciani was skilled in teaching these heady subjects in an engaging way that made him popular with the seminarians. He received his doctorate in sacred theology *magna cum laude* in 1947 from the Pontifical Gregorian University.

In 1958, Pope John XXIII appointed Luciani as Bishop of Vittorio Veneto, and he participated in all the sessions of the Second Vatican Council. In 1969, Pope Paul VI appointed him as the Patriarch of Venice, and elevated him as a cardinal in 1973. As bishop, Luciani was a staunch defender of Church doctrine, but his warm and humble style endeared him to his priests and to his people. A skilled orator and writer, Cardinal Luciani garnered a reputation as a champion for the poor and he emphasized holiness in his priests, rather than participation in the worker-priest movement.[7]

The new Pope John Paul I seemed to grasp immediately the importance of simple gestures that spoke volumes in an ancient office that is often viewed with jaded eyes. His double name honored his predecessors, with a subliminal nod to his desire to continue to reforms of the Second Vatican Council.

When John Paul addressed the crowds at the Angelus and during weekly audiences, he often departed from prepared remarks, and spoke directly from his heart to the people, disarming them with his gracious smile and his need to regularly adjust his *zucchetto* (skullcap) that always seemed slightly askew.

John Paul directed that the liturgy of his installation would not be the traditional coronation, but an "inauguration," with a simple bestowal of a bishop's pallium that symbolized a shepherd's service, rather than a tiara that was the last remnant of papal temporal power. He promised a revision of Canon Law and would take a good look at the structures and organization of the Roman Curia.

When a group of American bishops came to see him during their *Ad Limina* visit,[8] John Paul spoke with them about one of his favorite topics: the family as the "domestic church."

> What a wonderful thing it is when families realize the power they have for the sanctification of the world: the mutual sanctification of husband and wife and the reciprocal influence between parents and children. And then, by the loving witness of their lives, families can bring Christ's Gospel to others.[9]

And then on Friday morning of September 29, just 33 days after his election, good Pope John Paul was found dead in his room from an apparent heart attack.

Conclave deliberations are supposedly secret, but the smoke from the burning of ballots indicated that Albino Luciani was probably elected on the fourth ballot. This implied that there were a handful of names considered on the conservative and liberal sides, and Luciani was the compromise. Most likely, the cardinals did not want to just rehash in October what they deliberated on in August. It was also quite clear that the stress of the modern papacy might be too much for an older person. It had been more than 400 years since Adrian VI, the pope from the Netherlands. Was it time to break the Italian papal streak? Conclave watchers counted eight smoke events, but that does not necessarily mean there were eight ballots. Some of those later puffs might very well have been decoys to throw people off, if the rumors are true that Cardinal Wojtyla had requested some time in prayer to discern his election.

It was only when Cardinal Felice emerged on the balcony to announce *"Habemus papam"* that the white smoke was truly confirmed.

The name Wojtyla at first drew head scratching and puzzled looks that soon gave way to recognition and outright rejoicing. *"Un polaco!"* The College of Cardinals had done something historic and unprecedented. They gave the world a Polish pope!

Karol Josef Wojtyla was born on May 18, 1920 in Wadowice, a rural town in Poland where his father, also named Karol, served as a soldier in the local garrison. Young Karol's mother Emilia died in 1923 during childbirth. His older brother was a doctor who died in 1932 from an infection in the hospital where he worked.

As a young man in 1938, Karol moved to Krakow to study Polish literature at Jagiellonian University. It was a time of great promise, and Karol immersed himself in Polish culture, writing poetry, and getting involved in the Rhapsodic Theatre, a troupe of actors who specialized in romantic drama and heroic exploits from the Polish middle ages.

Karol was a playwright, and his talent for languages blossomed as he learned 11 languages in addition to his native Polish. This linguistic skill would serve him well as pope.

Then, in 1939, Karol's beloved homeland entered the darkest moment of its history. Nazi Germany invaded Poland on September 1. Sixteen days later, Russia joined the battle and the two powers carved up the conquered land between themselves. The Germans held the Poles in contempt as a slave race, and began a campaign to stamp out intellectual life.

In 1941, Karol's father died of a heart attack. "I was not at my mother's death, I was not at my brother's death, I was not at my father's death. At 20, I had already lost all the people I loved."[10] Shortly after, Karol began to seriously consider the priesthood.

Survival in wartime Poland was a daily challenge. Karol managed to stay alive by first working in a stone quarry and later in a chemical factory in Solvay.

At great personal risk, the Rhapsodic Theatre troupe continued in secret, performing in private apartments. Karol thus belonged to the "cultural resistance movement," prefiguring his opposition to Communism.

Karol disappeared from the Solvay factory in 1942, and was not heard from again until after the war. Karol had entered a secret seminary to study for the priesthood. The three seminaries of Krakow were suppressed, so Cardinal Adam Sapieha, Archbishop of Krakow, invited theology students into his roomy episcopal palace. Once inside, Karol and his four seminary companions could not emerge for fear of arrest.

Karol Wojtyla was ordained a priest on November 1, 1946. The Soviet Union tried, but soon found it impossible to drive a wedge between the Church and the people.

Father Wojtyla's talents were readily recognized, and in 1946, he was sent to Rome for two years of studies at the Angelicum University. His dissertation was entitled, "The Concept of Faith in the Writings of Saint John of the Cross," the mystic from Spain whom Wojtyla admired.

Returning to Poland, Wojtyla served two years as a parish priest in Niegowie and Krakow. In 1951, he started teaching moral theology at both Catholic University of Lublin, and at Krakow Seminary—even as he wrote poetry under the pseudonym, Andrzej Jawien. In 1958, Wojtyla was appointed Auxiliary Bishop of Krakow at age 38, the youngest member of the episcopacy. Six years later, he became the Archbishop of Krakow.

Archbishop Wojtyla was already well-known locally as a solid writer and professor of theology. Through his participation at the Second Vatican Council, he moved into the international scene. During the Council deliberations, he delivered interventions at the discussions on liturgy and revelation. He urged that the Church is best seen as the "People of God," and observers were impressed with the way he favored a more biblical and less clerical approach to the Church. He served on the commission that drafted the pivotal Vatican II document on *The Church in the Modern World (Gaudium et Spes)*.

Pope Paul VI elevated Wojtyla as a cardinal on June 26, 1967. Back home in his own diocese, such rank and honor were not important; anyone could see him. He was a friend of the students, and liked to go skiing and canoeing with them during holidays. They responded by calling him, "Uncle."

The complete story of Pope John Paul II, canonized as a saint in 2014, is beyond the scope of this book. Among his many accomplishments is the role he played in the downfall of Communism in Europe and the liberation of his beloved Poland. With his own eyes he saw more people—millions upon millions—than perhaps any other person in history through his landmark pastoral visits to more than 129 countries around the globe.

He founded World Youth Day, and endeared himself to millions of young people worldwide who flocked to the biennial international gatherings, bringing their enthusiasm and their contemporary music to the papal liturgies as Pope John Paul sang along with delight. On his final World Youth Day in Toronto in 2002, an older Pope John Paul's address to the young Church could very well be a reflection on his own remarkable life. *"People are made for happiness.* Rightly, then, you thirst for happiness. *Christ has the answer* to this desire of yours. But he asks you to trust him. *True joy is a victory,* something which cannot be obtained without *a long and difficult struggle.* Christ holds the secret of this victory."[11]

John Michael Talbot

In that unforgettable October of 1978, as winds of the Holy Spirit blew through the papal conclaves of the Catholic Church, that same Spirit was touching the heart of a remarkable young man. John Michael Talbot was composing songs that would appear on his breakthrough album, *The Lord's Supper.* Talbot remembers:

> As I settled into Alverna, I got used to living alone (which I had never done before), and I began to experience the rhythm of a liturgical day with the friars. It was at this time that new music emerged. It began as I read the missal that contained the words of the Mass. Soon songs were coming out as fast as I could sit down with my guitar to sing them.
>
> *The Lord's Supper* was originally conceived as a double album called *The Painter, Mass in the Key of D Major.* I recorded the entire body of songs at TRC recording in downtown Indianapolis. We originally tried putting drums and bass on after laying down the basic guitar and vocal, but it just didn't work, despite that being my usual process on two earlier Christian albums. We really didn't know what to do next.
>
> As I talked this through with Mark Clevenger, the engineer at TRC, Mark suggested that we try using singers from his new church, which was a community integrating Orthodox and Western Charismatic spirituality. We agreed, and the sessions continued.
>
> We used four to eight singers, and overdubbed them until they had some 400 voices recorded. It was a laborious and time-consuming process.
>
> The result was choral yet contemporary, classical yet charismatic. It was a musical expression of what I was going through spiritually and theologically as I inched my way into the Catholic Church.[12]

John Michael Talbot, the third child of Dick and Jamie Margaret Talbot, was born on May 8, 1954, in Oklahoma City. The three Talbot children—older brother Terry and sister Tanni—inherited musical talent from their grandfather, and they made a name for themselves as a young singing group, performing at school and local events as they moved from Oklahoma City to Little Rock, Arkansas, and Indianapolis.

"Music was a central feature of the Talbot's family life. Dick played the violin in the Oklahoma Symphony Orchestra, Jamie could frequently be found at the piano, and the three children would eventually pick up a score of instruments, ranging from tambourine to cello."[13] As they entered their teen years, Terry and John learned guitar and started a psychedelic band called Sounds Unlimited.

The Talbots were a Methodist family who attended church regularly. Dick Talbot served in the Army Air Corps during World War II, with assignments in India and Burma. Through this experience, he instilled in John a respect for all faiths and an openness to people of various cultures.

If you played guitar in the 1960s, you wanted to be a rock star, but only a select few could actually be one. Terry and John Talbot came close. Their band Mason Proffit was on an upward trajectory toward rock music stardom for four years.

Record producer Bill Trout suggested Terry and John ditch their old psychedelic trappings and find a new name and look. Inspired by Credence Clearwater Revival, they took on the name Mason Proffit Reunion, and shortened it later: "Mason" for its folksy feel, "Proffit" as an homage to Frank Proffit—the composer of the Kingston Trio hit, "Tom Dooley."

Mason Proffit had a gutsy folk sound that was underscored by the band's hard rock bass and drums. They had a unique sound that prefigured country rock, with a message of social conscience as they sang of equality, justice, and brotherly love.

Terry channeled his Methodist memories and brought a fiery preacher's energy to their set, working up the crowd into such a frenzy that the bands they opened for began to complain that Mason Proffit was stealing their thunder. The headliners they supported included Iron Butterfly, the Byrds, Fleetwood Mac, and the Grateful Dead. Along the way, their band charted several hits, including 'Two Hangmen' and 'A Thousand and Two.'

Looking back on those years, John recalled how the huge audiences that came to see Mason Proffit reminded him of the multitude who flocked to Jesus, who saw them as lost sheep. "There was an awful lot of dope, free lovemaking, nudity, drunkenness—I felt a deep caring and compassion for them. Even as I played and sang, even as I felt that old stage rush of adrenaline, I was at the same time stricken with a kind of grief."[14]

John became involved in a dizzying romance with a 19-year-old named Nancy. The band was living in a house in California, and John invited Nancy to move in with him. John's father would have none of that. Eventually, in 1971—near his 18th birthday—John and Nancy married at a Methodist church in Indianapolis.

"There was the glow and hope of a new start, but John soon realized that his inner search for truth was not satisfied. He felt more lost, alone and confused. Nancy sensed this and bluntly said, 'John, we've made a mistake. You should be a monk!'"[15]

The Talbot brothers always had a strong sense of the human spirit and social justice in the songs they wrote and performed. To those who knew them well, it was probably no surprise that they came to openly embrace the Christian faith. They decided to leave Mason Proffit. Their first album as a duo, while not overtly Christian, certainly had a strong Christian bent. Meanwhile, John became involved with the then-burgeoning Jesus Movement, but ultimately found the movement's fundamentalist leanings unfulfilling.

John became a voracious reader, and eventually discovered the writings of Saint John of the Cross, the mystic from Spain who founded monastic communities. And then he started reading Thomas Merton, the Trappist monk who expressed the need for meditation and contemplative prayer.

But searching inward does not pay the bills. John and Nancy just had a baby, and they had no steady source of income. Around this time, Terry called his brother and invited him to go on tour with a newly Christianized Mason Proffit. John would open up for them as a solo act. Through this tour, John met Billy Ray Hearn, an executive with Myrrh Records, a Christian label. Their fast friendship became the foundation of John's future success.

John's return to performing was causing new tensions in his marriage. For a while, he and Nancy hoped their new baby, Amy, might bring them closer together. Unexpressed expectations may have been a factor in their eventual decision to separate and then divorce. It was a difficult time for John, but he and Nancy remained friends.

John's journey led him to Alverna, a Franciscan retreat center only two miles from his parents' Indianapolis home. At Alverna, he met the Franciscan priest who would become his spiritual director.

> I had been reading about Saint Francis—about his incredible devotion to Christ and his stark, simple life that has always appealed to me. I could relate to the power of his conversion. And my other readings—books on the early church, the writings of Bernard of Clairvaux, Thomas à Kempis, Theresa of Avila, John of the Cross, and Thomas Merton—were all ministering so deeply to my spirit. Yet, I was troubled because they were all Catholic! I needed some understanding, and I thought that this Franciscan priest, Father Martin Wolter, could provide it.[16]

"John, I want you to think and pray about coming here to stay for a while," Father Martin ventured after several hours of intense conversation. "You need some space, some time to think, and a supportive environment—and you could study in the areas that interest you, such as Catholicism, community, and Franciscan spirituality."[17]

The priest recognized John's musical talent and encouraged it. Father Martin gave Talbot a steady diet of spiritual reading. He studied the writings of the early Church Fathers, as well as John Henry Newman, and other Christian mystics. Over the course of this intense experience of learning and prayer, Talbot's heart was changed. He decided to become a Catholic and was welcomed into the Church on Ash Wednesday, February 8, 1978, when he received conditional Baptism, Confirmation, and First Eucharist at Alverna's Upper Room Chapel.

New songs seemed to come quickly during his time before conversion. He prayed the official Mass texts and discovered how easily he could set them to music. This led to the recording of his landmark album, *The Lord's Supper,* which became an overwhelming bestseller among both Catholic and Protestant audiences.

Talbot reflected on the denominational bridge:

> I have addressed Evangelicals who have tried to reach Catholics and it can't be done. It's going to be artificial. You've got to be a Catholic to reach Catholics. There is something inherently intuitive in understanding the Catholic faith to do authentic Catholic music. Or at least you have to be liturgical or sacramental.

> Can it be bridged? I bridge it because it's who I am. It's my journey. I understand the Evangelicals. I understand Catholics, and it naturally happens with me. But it can't be imposed one way or the other without having to spend some time in the other camp authentically.[18]

Talbot started touring to promote his new music. To help his audiences understand the reality of his spiritual conversion, and to clearly distinguish himself from his former rock persona, he chose to perform while wearing the traditional brown habit of the Franciscan religious community. Talbot was a Third Order (lay) Franciscan, and was given permission to identify himself as such.[19]

While John Michael studied monasticism and lived in solitude with the Franciscans at Alverna, he was drawn to the idea of forming his own religious community.

> In the beginning, his dream for community flowed naturally from his life of prayer. The community was to be a support group of like-minded people, a base of operation that could facilitate the various functions of a multifaceted ministry. The focus would be on contemplative prayer rather than active ministry, so that both the life and the ministry of the community would be rooted in the power of Spirit-filled prayer.[20]

The new community would be known as the Little Portion House of Prayer, after the Portiuncula (little potion) of Saint Francis. Under the supervision of Father Martin, Talbot's new community took shape at the Alverna Retreat center. In 1980, he resettled his community in Eureka Springs, Arkansas, on land he had purchased during his days with Mason Proffit. This would become the Little Portion Hermitage and the Motherhouse of the Brothers and Sisters of Charity, as the community is formally known.

The Little Portion community struggled with its identity and purpose until they were joined by Sister Viola Pratka of the Incarnate Word community. She met Talbot at a concert with the Dallas Symphony Orchestra, and became intrigued with his fledgling community, joining them at their hermitage. With her 25 years of experience in religious life, she soon took up a leadership role, instilling much needed discipline and enthusiasm in the prayer life and work of the brothers and sisters. At Talbot's encouragement, Viola asked for and received dispensation from Rome so she could formally join the Brothers and Sisters of Charity.

Viola encouraged Talbot as he struggled with the writing of a "rule" for the community. He studied the rules of Saint Francis, Saint Benedict, and other monastic orders. Her suggestion: "John, just write from the Scriptures!" A Scripture Rule was drafted that gave new life and vision to the Little Portion Hermitage and a formal Constitution was adopted and received ecclesiastical approval. The Brothers and Sisters of Charity were on their way.

> We are a Catholic-based community of celibate brothers, celibate sisters, singles who can marry, and families, called as a monastic and domestic spiritual family into deep love relationships with and in Jesus Christ. We share common work and recreation areas while retaining appropriate separate cloistered areas for each expression. Our primary founder is Jesus, our primary rule is Scripture, and love is our primary law.[21]

And then, a surprising development. John and Viola announced their intention to be married. Canonically, all obstacles were cleared. John's first marriage had been annulled and his own private vows expired. Viola had already received dispensation from Rome from the vows to her previous religious order. After much discernment, prayer and advice from their spiritual advisors, John Michael Talbot married Viola Pratka in a quiet ceremony at Charity Chapel at Little Portion Hermitage on February 17, 1989. Bishop Andrew J. McDonald of the Diocese of Little Rock presided. Through their sacramental union, John and Viola give loving witness that marriage can work within the structure of a religious community.

In December 1991, John Michael and Viola had the privilege of meeting with Pope John Paul II while they were at the Vatican to discuss the establishment of their community. They were invited to celebrate early morning Eucharist with him in his private chapel.

"When we were escorted into the chapel by the Swiss Guard, there were about 30 people there," Talbot remembered.

> Pope John Paul was already kneeling in front, deep in prayer. The sisters assisted with his vestments and then Mass began. The sacred silence was astounding.[22]

> Finally, it was time for Communion. We filed out of our row of seats toward the Holy Father. I was about to receive Communion from the Vicar of Christ and the successor of Saint Peter. My knees trembled—I was overwhelmed.

It was then that I realized that it was something even greater than this that occurs at every Mass. It is Jesus himself who is present in the Eucharist, not merely his servant. I learned many lessons I thought I had already learned without a word being said at that liturgy.[23]

John Michael Talbot has enjoyed a prolific career, releasing more than 50 albums of worship music with multi-platinum sales, and more than 30 books of meditations and prayer, Scriptural reflections and pastoral titles such as *The Joy of Music Ministry*. He and Viola have traveled the world through concert tours, speaking at conferences, parish missions, and leading pilgrimages to the Holy Land and other sacred sites. He is host of an inspirational television program, *All Things Are Possible* on the Church Channel, broadcast by the Trinity Broadcasting Network. The Brothers and Sisters of Charity is a thriving religious community with two monastic homes: Little Portion Hermitage in Berryville, Arkansas, and Saint Clare Monastery in Houston, Texas.

Talbot's music has been blessed with interdenominational popularity and is sung at praise and worship events, Charismatic conferences, and retreat weekends. He also has several songs that have become favorites in Catholic liturgy, including "Come, Worship the Lord," "I Am the Bread of Life," "Only in God," and "Holy Is His Name," a beloved meditative setting of the Magnificat, Mary's song of praise.[24] With its soaring melody, this song truly expresses the remarkable journey of John Michael Talbot.

---

[1]   Hebblethwaite, Peter, *The Year of Three Popes*. (Cleveland: Collins, 1978) 114.

[2]   Stourton, Edward, *John Paul II: Man of History*. London: Hodder & Stoughton (2006), 171.

[3]   Editorial, "Pope Paul at the United Nations: An Historic Day," *America: The National Catholic Review*. October 16, 1965.

[4]   *Address of the Holy Father Paul VI To The United Nations Organization*, Monday, 4 October 1965. *Libreria Editrice Vaticana*, per Vatican website.

[5]   Editorial, "Pope Paul VI: 1963-1978," *America: The National Catholic Review*. August 19, 1978.

[6]   "The Life of Albino Luciani," The Pope John Paul I Association.

[7]   The Worker-Priest movement was a missionary initiative, popular especially in France, that encouraged priests to work in factories and other places of employment to experience the everyday life of the working-class people whom they served.

[8]   Ad Limina visit is the obligatory duty of diocesan bishops and certain territorial prelates (e.g., abbots) to visit the tombs of Saints Peter and Paul and to meet with the pope to report on the state of their dioceses or prelatures. In modern times, bishops are required to fulfill an Ad Limina visit every five years.

[9]   Pope John Paul I, "Address to Group of Visiting U.S. Bishops," September 21, 1978.

[10] Stourton, Edward, *John Paul II: Man of History*. London: Hodder & Stoughton (2006), 60.

[11] Pope John Paul II, Welcoming Address, World Youth Day, Toronto, Canada, 2002. http://saltandlighttv.org/blogfeed/getpost.php?id=38447

[12] O'Neill, Dan, *Signatures: The Story of John Michael Talbot* (Berryville, AR: Messenger Communications, Inc., and Little Portion, Inc., 1983) 124-125.

[13] Ibid., 16.

[14] Ibid., 55.

[15] Ibid., 32.

[16] Ibid., 81-82.

[17] Ibid., 84.

[18] Interview with the author, August 30, 2013 in Anaheim, California. Talbot did start an organization called Catholic Association of Musicians (CAM) to give support to Catholic musicians in the model of CCM. But it met with limited success because of apparent reluctance by established Catholic publishers and composers to come on board.

[19] "There are three orders of Saint Francis: the First Order, or the Order of Friars Minor, who are celibate, vowed men. The Second Order is comprised of cloistered nuns, or "Poor Clares," as they are sometimes called, after the first Franciscan sister. The Third Order is subdivided into vowed and non-vowed brothers and sisters,

as well as married couples, and diocesan clergy, who seek to follow the example of the saint from Assisi, either in community or in private homes." See O'Neill, 117.

[20] O'Neill, 131-132.

[21] See website of the Brothers and Sisters of Charity at Little Portion Hermitage Monastery: https://littleportion.org

[22] Interview with the author, August 30, 2013 in Anaheim, California.

[23] O'Neill, 207.

[24] Luke 1:46-55.

Chapter Eleven

"On Eagle's Wings"
NALR Expands and Diversifies

The prayers at Camp David were the same as those of the shepherd King David, who prayed in the 85th Psalm, "Wilt thou not revive us again: that thy people may rejoice in thee?... I will hear what God the Lord will speak: for he will speak peace unto his people, and unto his saints: but let them not return again unto folly."

-President Jimmy Carter, address before a Joint Session
of Congress on the Camp David meeting regarding
the Middle East, September 18, 1978

Arizona is young and daring. She is not tied to precedent, to convention, to other states' ways of doing things. She is bent on making her own ways, and in her own way. Her mistakes will be her own, and her triumphs likewise.

-George Wharton James, *Arizona, the Wonderland*, 1917

NALR was riding high in 1977. They had gambled on untested composers and it paid off handsomely. Part of it was the sheer luck of being in the right place at the right time with composers on the cusp of a breakthrough. They also had a good sense of marketing and salesmanship. How would NALR capitalize on its success?

Ray Bruno and Dan Onley observed the popularity of *Hymnal for Young Christians*, FEL's bestselling series, and the tremendous sales of World Library's *Peoples Mass Book*. NALR decided to publish a similar compilation songbook (they didn't use the word "hymnal" yet) that featured their own popular composers. It was Bob Lesinski of NALR Sales who suggested a title, based on a familiar St. Louis Jesuits song: *Glory & Praise*.

Their 1973 song supplement, *SING PRAISE*, gave NALR a head start compiling *Glory & Praise*. "Once the concept was approved, Dan Onley put together that first volume fairly quickly," remembers Erich Sylvester.[1] Published in 1977, *Glory & Praise* was a relatively thin booklet, but the 80 songs were among the most popular in the mid-1970s: "Be Not Afraid" (Dufford), "Blest Be the Lord" (Schutte), "Dwelling Place" (Foley), "Only a Shadow" (Landry), "Seek the Lord" (O'Connor), and more. The presentation was rather simple: no foreword, with the songs in alphabetical order, followed by a few Mass settings, plus a basic index in the back.

Despite this modest beginning, *Glory & Praise* became a bestseller. Its 1977 release coincided with FEL's high-profile litigation with the Archdiocese of Chicago, which catapulted copyright awareness into the forefront of discussion among pastors and diocesan worship offices. NALR's professionally printed songbook solved many problems on the parish level, including copyright compliance.

Glory & Praise was originally released with a guitar accompaniment edition, plus a pew edition with the melody and words for the assembly. By popular demand, a keyboard edition was released in 1979—a major style crossover breakthrough.

Glory & Praise, Volume 2 appeared in 1980, and contained 92 songs numbered (81-173) to preserve continuity with the first volume. It also became a bestseller. Volume 3 was released in 1982 and featured 101 songs (numbered 174-275), offering the most recent songs of veteran composers, plus newcomers to NALR who were having an impact around the country: the Dameans, the Monks of Weston Priory, Ellis & Lynch, and Jesuit Father Bob Fabing. In 1983, NALR published a combined edition of all three *Glory & Praise* volumes that proved popular with the company's loyal audience.

The year 1984 saw the release of a specialty edition, *Young People's Glory & Praise,* edited by Carey Landry and Carol Jean Kinghorn, and featuring a selection of their *Hi God* songs, plus music by Jack Miffleton, Harry Pritchett, and other children's composers. It included standards of the contemporary repertoire that were favorites of grade school kids: "The King of Glory," "On Eagle's Wings," "Sing, Alleluia, Sing," "Glory and Praise to Our God," and more.

In 1987, NALR and GIA jointly published an ambitious hardcover edition of *Glory & Praise* that included the Order of Mass, new composers such as Tom Kendzia, Grayson Warren Brown and Rory Cooney, plus works by GIA stalwarts Marty Haugen and David Haas. *Glory & Praise* would continue into the 21st century.

In his book, *The History of American Catholic Hymnals Since Vatican II,* Marianist Brother Donald Boccardi made this observation on the first volume of *Glory & Praise.* "There is no way to exaggerate the influence of this short collection and the other volumes that were to follow it."[2] As the 1970s progressed, NALR grew its roster with several influential composers.

The Dameans

The early story of the Dameans includes three albums for FEL Publications, and a ministry that enriched the Folk Mass repertoire with songs that became parish standards in the late 60s and early 70s: "Look Beyond," "Shout Out Your Joy," "The New Creation," and so much more. But after almost 10 years of recording and touring, the quintet discovered they were not receiving their promised royalties. They took their publisher to court in their home town, Baton Rouge, Louisiana.[3]

In 1979, the landmark royalty case, *Ault vs. FEL Publications,* was resolved in an out-of-court settlement. The Dameans received from FEL full ownership of their copyrights and master tapes. Gary Ault, Buddy Ceasar, Mike Balhoff, Darryl Ducote, and Dave Baker were now free to map out their own course in a brave new liturgical music world. But Baker decided to leave the group, wishing his longtime friends well in their new endeavors.

Their first step was to return to the studio and re-record their early songs, revising the lyrics to reflect the increasing sensitivity to inclusive language. For example, in their popular Communion song, "Look Beyond," the first verse was changed from "Our fathers brought us manna from the sky" to "Moses brought us manna from the sky."

Gary Ault recalled, "We were trying to get a publisher for the next record, *Beginning Today*. We contacted Teleketics – that's Franciscan Communications in Los Angeles. We made one record with them and it just didn't work out. It wasn't profitable. They owned all of *Beginning Today*. That's the only record in our history that we did not own, after we got everything back from FEL."[4]

The Dameans decided to record new songs plus a Mass setting for an album that was eventually called *Day of the Sun*. But they were on their own now, and they needed a new record producer. A cousin of Ault's was married to a studio owner who was a partner with legendary New Orleans maestro Allen Toussaint. The Rock and Roll Hall of Famer advised Ault to see Wardell Quezergue, another legend who produced such local acts as the Neville Brothers, and Dr. John. Wardell's laid-back manner was both appealing and puzzling.

Ault continued the story:

> So, I had to go back and report to the Dameans that I had this guy who said he can do it and 'Don't worry about the cost or what it's going to sound like because you *will* like it.' And the guys gave me these strange looks. 'What are you getting us into now?' Long story short, we get into the studio and—he is a genius, he is a gentleman! And we ended up having a long-standing relationship on several records with Wardell. And that is how we got into doing things on our own. And after we got real good doing that, then we went to NALR.[5]

But before the group went to Phoenix, the Dameans welcomed a new member, who brought fresh energy to the group. "After Dave left, the four of us did *Beginning Today*," Ault remembered. "When we got into *Day of the Son*, Mike Balhoff knew a talented kid in his parish, Gary Daigle, and invited him to be part of our music ministry.

> Gary Daigle was a paid musician for a number of years. When we decided to make him an official part of the Dameans, I told him, 'You're not just a paid employee anymore. Now you are responsible for all our debts with us,'" Ault said with a laugh.[6]

In addition to singing, Daigle brought a new dynamic to the Dameans as a musician and songwriter. His piano arrangement on "We Praise You" was influenced by the soaring piano on Simon & Garfunkel's "Bridge Over Troubled Water." He took the basic rhythm but utilized new chords that, in turn, inspired the direction of the song.

"Mike had written out the verses. As soon as I hit the four chords before the verse, I just let it go and Darryl began to sing. And the melody almost came instantly. That was just an extension of the way they had written prior to my joining. I think what I brought was an added vocabulary of chord progressions and styles."[7]

The Dameans produced several albums with NALR. *Remember Your Love* featured some memorable moments:

> When we finished 'We Praise You,' we were just quiet. We left the studio with a cassette, and played it in the car on the way to our place. We knew that something special just happened, with Wardell's arrangements and the lush strings. It was great. And that collection was the first time we did a concept album, where we took psalms and made them into songs. 'Speak, Lord, I'm Listening' was on the album. It came from a youth conference in New Orleans, where we were commissioned to do the theme song. Must have been 40,000 young people. We did that with full band at the Super Dome. It was a great experience.[8]

Path of Life was one of the first contemporary collections with music dedicated to RCIA. The album's liner notes reveal the intentions of the composers.

> This album was specifically designed to aid in the celebration of the faith journey called the "catechumenate." In the early Church, this was the process of search and conversion experienced by those who sought membership in the Christian community through baptism.

After more than 10 albums and 100 songs, the Dameans moved on to their private lives. Gary Ault devoted himself to teaching and working with young people. Darryl Ducote became a clinical social worker. Michael Balhoff worked in the telecommunications industry, and Buddy Caesar earned a doctorate in counseling. Gary Daigle went on to a prolific career as a liturgical composer with GIA. As lifelong friends, the Dameans and their families try to get together regularly and do occasional reunion concerts—their signature vocal blend still as mesmerizing as when they sang at the seminary all those years ago.

Grayson Warren Brown

"When I was 15 years old," Grayson Warren Brown remembered,

> I went to work for a parish called Saint Ann's in a small black and Hispanic community [in Brooklyn, New York]. This was at the very beginning of the civil rights movement of the 60s. A number of very fortunate things happened to me. One was that we had a clerical staff that was very interested in making Saint Ann's a place where people could come and really experience liturgy. Back then there was very little in the way of music and prayer for black people.
>
> One thing the priests there encouraged all of us to do was to create. Their attitude was that there simply isn't enough happening that reflects either the culture of the people here or that affects the whole idea of justice, which was so relevant to us at that time—and still is, I hope. They encouraged us to look within ourselves and find our own talents and bring them to the surface.

It certainly moved me from an organist, which is what I intended to be, to someone who became involved in the whole liturgical scheme of things. I was rather surprised to find that the Church as a whole did not operate that way. I would say my experience at Saint Ann's really set me on the road to what I'm doing today.[9]

The priests at Grayson's parish were invited to attend an event with Dr. Martin Luther King at Riverside Church in Manhattan and they brought their young organist with them.

Dr. King spoke for about an hour and then took questions from the audience. After the meeting was over, people were invited to shake Dr. King's hand. I was a young man, maybe 18 or 19 years old, and I believe the only teenager in the room. Much to my surprise, I was also one of the few African Americans.

I will never forget the moment when I went up to shake Dr. King's hand. He looked at me and his face lit up. He gave me a big smile and said, 'Well, hello!' What an experience for me, a young black teenager, to be able to meet the man who already was a hero of mine and would have the greatest impact in my spiritual life in ways that, at the time, I could never have imagined.

There was another legendary person who had a profound influence on Brown's life:

I also owe some thanks to Reverend Clarence Joseph Rivers. He was, in 1966, a young black priest from the Archdiocese of Cincinnati, and he wrote and recorded a Mass entitled *The American Mass Program*. For its time, it was absolutely revolutionary. It wasn't what one could call gospel music, at least how we define gospel music today; it was more akin to the old Negro spirituals that many of us grew up hearing. When I was young, being able to sing Father Rivers' music at Saint Ann was truly liberating and quite moving.

It was after hearing this music that I began to think I might write some music as well. Of course, the majority of people I mentioned this to told me I was nuts, which was not at all that unreasonable considering I had never written a piece of music in my entire life.

Then, one day, I was invited to attend the Liturgical Conference which was being held that year in Chicago. At the conference, I met Father Rivers and got to play one of my compositions for him. He told me it was very good and said that he had just started a publishing company. He told me I needed to find a way to make a recording and that he knew a few people in the Catholic music business. If I got a recording made, he would call them and get me in the door.[10]

The song that Grayson played for Father Rivers was from his newly composed *Mass for a Soulfull People*,[11] that he premiered at Saint Benedict Church in Washington, DC, the parish of Brown's friend, Valencia Rogers—a gifted singer associated with the

Howard University Gospel Choir, who sang at the premiere.

"Someone taped the concert on an old reel-to-reel and gave me a copy," Brown remembered:

> Everyone who heard the Mass told me I had a hit on my hands and should do a professional recording. That was going to cost me about $5,000. To me, a 20-year-old inner city kid who lived in the projects, it was like saying I needed $50 million. I tried, but after months of trying, the best I could do was raise $2,200. It looked as though my dream of doing a recording was going to die.[12]

The young composer was discouraged, but he continued with his music ministry. In 1968, the Diocese of Brooklyn was celebrating the ordination and installation of its new ordinary, Bishop Francis Mugavero. Grayson was tapped to serve as a cantor. He led the closing hymn, "Battle Hymn of the Republic," with fire and gusto. The bishop was clearly impressed and he sang along heartily with his new people.

Brown thought he would visit Bishop Mugavero and seek his support. "I called the bishop's office and spoke to his secretary. I explained that I was the young man who had led the singing at the Mass in the cathedral the night before the bishop's ordination. I asked if it would be possible to have a meeting with the bishop and share a project I was working on. Much to my surprise, I was able to have that meeting."[13]

Grayson's nervousness about the meeting was compounded by his lugging a heavy reel-to-reel tape recorder to the chancery, so he could play his Mass setting for the bishop.

> He seemed to enjoy the music. He enjoyed even more the reaction he heard from the congregation, who was clapping joyfully and singing with the music. He asked me how much money I had raised, and I told him $2,200; $2,800 short of my goal. He turned to me and said, 'Okay, I'll give you the $2,800.' I was stunned! With the $5,000, I was able to go to Washington, and with the help of the Howard University Gospel Choir, I recorded my first album.[14]

That first album, *Hymns for a Soulfull People*, was picked up for distribution in 1977 by NALR, who designed a distinctive cover featuring African American ministers in liturgical procession. It became a bestselling groundbreaker, and was praised by renowned Gospel artist Edwin Hawkins. "I enjoyed listening to Grayson Brown's *A Mass for a Soulfull People*. It's good, inspiring music and should add a new dimension of soul to the Catholic liturgy."[15]

Brown would go on to produce several popular albums with NALR and OCP, including *I Will Rejoice, Been So Busy, If God Is for Us,* and *Greatness and Glory Are Yours.* He continues to compose, and his most recent collection is *Praise the Lord in Many Voices.* He has written three books: *God's Liberating Justice, Jesusgate,* and *The Transformative Power of Faith.* He is in much demand as a workshop presenter at parishes and conferences, and has led international pilgrimages to Africa and Ireland.

Grayson Warren Brown is an untiring advocate for multicultural inclusion in the Catholic Church. He has served on the Culture and Worship Advisory Committee for the National Office for Black Catholics, and on many other organizations.

> This whole adventure taught me something about faith. It is this: opportunity will often give you a narrow passageway to navigate through in order to take full use of that opportunity, but it will also offer wide corridors you can sail through toward failure. The key to navigating that narrow passageway toward success is faith. You've got to believe.[16]

Bob Fabing, SJ

Born in 1942, Robert Fabing learned to play the guitar in high school, and formed his own folk group that toured the San Francisco area during the heyday of The Kingston Trio. He joined the Jesuits in 1960, and started teaching at Loyola High School in 1966, doing occasional liturgies and concerts with Folk Mass composer Sebastian Temple, who lived near the campus.

After ordination to the priesthood, Father Fabing began an eight-year doctoral program in counseling, psychology, and the integration of psychotherapy and spiritual direction. Bob Fabing became involved in music ministry at the Oakland cathedral, and was inspired to compose his signature song, "Be Like the Sun," plus "The Gift," and other songs. This caught the attention of the new music division at Alba House Communications in Canton, Ohio, a ministry of the Paulist Fathers.

In 1974, Fabing recorded his first Alba album, *Be Like the Sun.* He toured widely and promoted his music including a 40-year string of consecutive appearances at the Los Angeles Religious Education Congress in Anaheim. Fabing went on to record several albums with NALR, including *Song to the Lamb, Winter Risen* and *Everlasting Covenant.* He is now published by OCP.

One unique aspect of Fabing's music is the way it springs from his non-liturgical ministry. He founded the Jesuit Institute for Family Life International Network, establishing 76 marriage counseling and family therapy centers worldwide. The Institute offers a blend of spiritual direction along with counseling in marriage, family, individual, and group settings. Fabing generally does not compose for the needs of the liturgy. "My songs come from my prayer," said Fabing. "I don't write out of any liturgical need. I recognize from my prayer with Christ how deeply people need to pray, and how people are hungry for music that will bring them to prayer. I'm writing out of the need of families and people who feel so destroyed, and for priests and sisters who don't know how to pray."[17]

Fabing established the 30-day Silent Retreat at El Retiro Jesuit Retreat Center in Los Altos, California. In 1978, a brother of the Missionaries of Charity participated in one of those retreats, and was so moved by the experience that he recommended Fabing to his community. This led to a long association with Mother Teresa.

Fabing has cherished memories of his encounters with the founder of the Missionaries of Charity:

> I first met Mother Teresa in 1984 in Calcutta. There were no airs about her at all; you would think you were talking with your grandmother. We were introduced and because she had just come home, she talked excitedly for 20 minutes. Then she said, "Oh, Father. Who are you? Tell me about yourself." I told her about the Jesuit Institute for Family Life and my work in spiritual direction and music. She let me tell my story, and then offered some thoughtful insight.
>
> "You know, Father, your job is harder than mine."
>
> "What do you mean, Mother?"
>
> "The poverty you deal with is deeper than the poverty I serve. I can take a bowl of rice downstairs out into the streets in Calcutta and give it to someone, and they look up at me and say, 'Oh, Mother. Thank you, thank you!' It's harder for you to get a smile out of people. The work you do in counseling married couples is harder than mine."[18]

When she died in 1997, Fabing, before a global television audience, sang the song he wrote for the gentle nun who had inspired the world.

> May your grace make me whole again.
> May your eyes make me see again.
> May your words make me hear again
> your song of love.[19]
> ©1984, OCP.

He composed *Mass for Teresa of Calcutta* for her canonization and continues to serve as chaplain for the community's novitiate in San Francisco.

Tom Kendzia

Tom Kendzia recalls fondly the roots of his chosen career as a composer:

> Liturgy and music have always been a part of my life since childhood. I attended Catholic school, often testing the patience of the Sisters of Mercy, and served as an altar boy in the neighborhood parish, learning Latin responses in the days before Vatican II. My mother, who was French Canadian, had a strong devotion to Saint Anne; my father, part Irish, to Saint Patrick. Like many families of that time, we prayed together often, and our home was decorated by religious art. Each of these three environments—home, school, and parish—has influenced my work as a liturgical musician.
>
> Our parish was lucky enough to have a decent pipe organ, an active and talented choir, and a choir director who understood how important music was to the liturgy. We didn't have a children's choir, so there was no real opportunity for me to be involved in the music at church.

Soon after, however, Vatican II encouraged variety in music at liturgy, and our parish held its first guitar Mass. I could now participate in the music at church. Because of my enthusiasm, I was able to help lead the group. This was a very big deal for me, a seventh grader at the time. My guitar playing continued through high school.

It was during this time that I was able to experience the power of music at liturgy. At the end of a retreat weekend for high school juniors and seniors, we gathered for the closing liturgy. Our singing was led by one priest with a guitar. But because of all the prayer, talk, and activities at the retreat, when we sang together it became apparent that we were one body without the usual fears and peer pressures of teenagers. The face of Christ could clearly be seen in the midst of the singing.[20]

Tom recorded a demo of the liturgical songs he composed at his Rhode Island parish. He thought about where he would submit it. Not GIA, with its more traditional vibe. Not FEL, which was obviously in decline. He sent it to WLP (World Library), and to NALR, which was really the only viable Catholic publisher in the 1970s committed to contemporary music. Several months after he submitted his work, he heard nothing.

The NPM convention in 1979 announced a contest for aspiring composers. The prize was the opportunity to perform in front of all those pastoral musicians from around the country. Kendzia submitted his music to the contest. To his everlasting surprise, he won!

That caught the attention of Paul Quinlan, Artists & Repertoire head at NALR. He remembered Kendzia's name, dug through the piles of submissions on his desk, and listened again to Tom's demo. He gave the young composer a call. "I'll be there at NPM and I'd be happy to meet with you after your performance." After Tom's Chicago performance, Quinlan met with him backstage and said, "We would like to do a project with you."

Kendzia was excited about this opportunity. He was an admirer of the St. Louis Jesuits and modeled his music on the sound he heard on their *Earthen Vessels* album.[21] The titles of his songs certainly sounded liturgical: "For Your Love," "Make Us One," and "Send Us Your Spirit."

When Tom arrived in Phoenix, Quinlan threw him a curveball. "I think Ray wants something more hip. Can you liven this stuff up?"

"What do you mean?" said Tom, puzzled.

"Well, let's get drums and electric guitars and bass and do a more rock version of your music."

"Oh. Okay." said Tom, scratching his head. This was not at all on his radar.[22]

Ray Bruno had a dream of bringing Catholic music to the same level as the secular recording industry. He joined the National Academy of Recording Arts and Sciences (NARAS) specifically to network with industry executives and nominate NALR records for the Grammy Awards. He saw in Tom Kendzia the potential to finally bridge that gap between sacred and secular.

This vision is consistent with Bruno's intentions since the early 1970s, when he broke off from World Library and started Epoch Records. "A bridge has got to be built between the secular and religious industries," Bruno said in *Billboard* magazine. "Our sound is equally as professional as that of secular artists, and our range of styles just as broad."[23]

Kendzia was young, and he was amazed at the funds that Bruno generously poured into his recording, enabling him to realize his music in ways he never dreamed possible. His first album, *Light of the World,* was polished and professional. An NALR promotional write-up describes:

> a contemporary pop sound reminiscent of a Broadway show. It is a combination of different styles ranging from upbeat jazz to slow ballads. Even the ballads have the raw energy characteristic of rock music. Tom describes the album as 'a journey through different styles that express different aspects of spiritual commitment.'[24]

Tom remembers going on the road to promote his new album. "I was on tour with a great rock and roll band. We were doing concerts, and in some places, the response was spectacular! In other places the audience looked at each other and said 'What the hell was that?'" [25] For the Catholic audience, *Light of the World* was clearly ahead of its time.

Despite the album's mixed reception, Tom Kendzia impressed Ray Bruno. When Paul Quinlan left the company, Tom became NALR's producer. He moved to Phoenix, and put together some fine albums with Rory Cooney, Bob Fabing, Cyprian Consiglio, and other artists.

Kendzia moved on from NALR and returned to his liturgical roots, recording more than 30 collections of music, mostly with OCP, including *Lead Us to the Water, Clothed in Love,* and *Endless Is Your Love.* His popular songs include "I, the Lord," "Now Is the Time," "Stand by Me," and "The Eyes and Hands of Christ," featured in today's hymnals and missals. Tom travels widely, presenting concerts and workshops throughout the United States, Canada, Europe, Asia and the Caribbean, with annual appearances in Ireland.

Michael Joncas

Born in Minneapolis, Minnesota in 1951, Jan Michael Joncas is the son of Paul Eugene Joncas, a theatre-arts professional, and Theresa Janine (Narog) Joncas, a lyric soprano who gave up a career as a professional singer to raise eight children, of whom Michael is the oldest. He remembered his early memories of music in the liturgy:

> My involvement with liturgical music really began in early childhood, listening to the chant and polyphony sung and played at the three parishes I was taken to by my parents and grandparents. My mother sang solos occasionally at All Saints Catholic Church in Northeast Minneapolis where I was exposed to Polish devotional music such as the Christmas *kalendy.*

At Saint Lawrence Church in Southeast Minneapolis, I was exposed to devotional music. Moving to Saint Charles Borromeo in Northeast Minneapolis for the rest of grade school, I encountered a parish with a strong Sunday adult choral program with a serviceable organ. I received from the Sisters of Saint Joseph who taught in the school there, an opportunity to be part of a funeral choir. They introduced me to Gelineau psalmody which was the 'cutting edge' of liturgical composition in the 1950s. I also had weekly piano lessons.[26]

Joncas was a "lifer" who entered seminary right after grade school. In 1965, he entered Nazareth Hall high school seminary, matriculated to Saint John Vianney college seminary, and received a bachelor's degree from the University of Saint Thomas. He took three years off and worked at Saint Joseph Church in New Hope, Minnesota, as liturgy and music director, returning to Saint Paul Seminary for theological studies. He was ordained a priest for the Archdiocese of Saint Paul and Minneapolis in 1980.

During his youth, Joncas' father worked as a stagehand for the Metropolitan Opera, and would sneak his son backstage to hear stunning performances of classical composers.

Sister Stanley, my piano teacher, had an inkling that I might be interested in composition, because she assigned me the progressive volumes of Bela Bartok's *Mikrokosmos*. The result of all this was that I began writing my own compositions in late grade school, and by mid-high school had won the Minnesota Young Composers contest twice in my age group—for a piano piece, and for a sonatina for violin and piano.[27]

Joncas' third stream of music education came from popular music. "I fell in love with the balladry of Peter, Paul & Mary, Joan Baez, Judy Collins, Bob Dylan, and Joni Mitchell, and taught myself guitar in order to sing this repertoire."[28] All these influences came together in the music he would compose for liturgy.

Joncas composed an early collection of liturgical music, *Singing in the Light,* released by World Library on the week of his graduation from the high school seminary, but it was unknown due to lack of promotion. Ten years later, he submitted to NALR the songs that would appear on his groundbreaking album, *On Eagle's Wings.* "In some ways, that collection illustrates the kinds of liturgical music we were singing in the late 1970s."[29]

Erich Sylvester remembers when he first heard Joncas' submission. "He sent us a quarter-inch tape, a complete production. I put it on and listened to it. The very first song was 'On Eagle's Wings.' I went to Ray and Dan and said, 'You must put this out. This is absolutely first-rate! Beautiful! This is a very talented composer, and you must publish him.' And, of course, they did."[30]

On Eagle's Wings had an immediate impact on churches, pastoral musicians, and music critics. The poetically expressed scriptural lyrics, the warm and appealing melodies, and the sophisticated approach to composition were very striking. The title song became an international classic, beloved by choirs and congregations across all Christian denominations.

Joncas produced two more collections with NALR: *Here in Our Midst* (1983) and *O Joyful Light* (1985). He released *Every Stone Shall Cry* in 1982 with Cooperative Ministries, an independent label comprised of non-published composers, subsequently re-released by OCP. Inspired by his friendship with Marty Haugen and David Haas, Joncas released several collections with GIA: *God of Life and of the Living* (1988), *The Winter Name of God* (1988), and the ambitious *No Greater Love* (1988)—an attempt to craft an "orchestral" Mass inspired by those of Mozart, Haydn and Schubert, but written according to the specifications of the reformed liturgy.

Uniquely, Joncas is published by a variety of publishers, with 20 collections of music and counting. "I long ago decided to live on my salary as a diocesan priest," Joncas explains:

"The royalties I receive go into a trust fund whose trustee determines what can be used to support my physical, emotional or spiritual well-being, as well as what is disbursed to charities."[31]

In the midst of his very busy schedule as a priest and composer, Joncas graduated *summa cum laude* from the University of Notre Dame with a master's in theology and liturgical studies. He also studied at the Pontificio Instituto Liturgico of the Ateneo Sant'Anselmo in Rome, where he earned a licentiate and doctorate in sacred liturgy. He has published several books, written more than 100 articles, and is in much demand as a lecturer at liturgical conferences and institutes around the world. At this writing, he serves as an Artist-in-Residence and Research Fellow in Catholic Studies at the University of Saint Thomas in Saint Paul, Minnesota.

Father Joncas' life was shattered in April 2003 when he was diagnosed with a neurological disorder known as Guillain-Barré Syndrome, a condition in which the body's immune system attacks part of the peripheral nervous system. Joncas was hospitalized and in therapy for more than a year. Thanks to an excellent course of medical treatment, and to the outpouring of prayers and support from family and friends, Joncas recovered. His courageous story is told in his book, *On Eagle's Wings: A Journey through Illness toward Healing* (Twenty-Third Publications, ©2017).

Michael Joncas eventually returned to teaching, composing, and priestly ministry, with renewed vigor. His most recent compositions reflect the deepening spirituality that resulted from his life-changing encounter with serious illness. He is an inspiration, not only for pastoral musicians and students of liturgy, but for all who have experienced chronic illness themselves or who have cared for a loved one who suffers.

·■·

In the late 1970s, NALR was starting to get noticed in the media, with write-ups in music industry trade journals, and in the business sections of newspapers. Million-dollar sales projections make people sit up and take notice. It was amazing to think that sales of this magnitude could be generated in the supposedly "niche" market of Catholic liturgical music.

> In seven years, Ray Bruno of North American Liturgy Resources in Phoenix has boosted his annual gross revenues from approximately $70,000 in 1971 to a projected $4 million in 1978.

With a largely Roman Catholic market, NALR produces contemporary music for worship aimed at the 18,000 Catholic church communities in the US. More recently, because of vastly improved productions, the wider market of general Christian listeners has been turning on to the characteristically scriptural lyric and folk-based style of NALR's family of recording artists. Thirteen of the firm's 60 releases are new for 1978.[32]

Carey Landry and the St. Louis Jesuits began the wave of success for NALR in the early 1970s. By decade's end, a whole cohort of newly discovered composers was poised to continue the company's good fortune. The enormously popular *Glory & Praise* series was another part of this success, ensuring that NALR's copyrights would be sung in America's churches every Sunday. In a very real and tangible way, that kind of weekly song exposure into the hearts and voices of faithful congregants was even more powerful than Top 40 radio play.

Bruno paid for an expensive promotional section in *Billboard,* the record industry's international newsweekly, to help build the perception of NALR's success among the publication's lucrative and influential industry readership. Featured in the September 27, 1980, issue of *Billboard,* the section is a fascinating window into NALR's hopes and dreams for the new decade, featuring photos and stories on their impressive roster of composers, along with articles on NALR Vice-President David Serey and on Bruno himself. Despite this optimism for the future, a storm was brewing that would make the 1974 "Super Outbreak" tornadoes in Cincinnati pale in comparison.

---

[1] Interview with the author, June 30, 2017, via telephone from San Francisco, California.

[2] Boccardi, SM, STD, Bro. Donald, The History of American Catholic Hymnals Since Vatican II, (Chicago, IL: GIA Publications, Inc., 2001) 70.

[3] The complete story of *Ault vs. FEL Publications* is told in Canedo, Ken, *Keep the Fire Burning: The Folk Mass Revolution* (Portland, OR: Pastoral Press, 2009) 129-130.

[4] Interview with the author, April 27, 2011 in New Orleans, Louisiana.

[5] Ibid.

[6] Ibid.

[7] Interview with the author, January 24, 2018 in St. Louis, Missouri.

[8] Ibid.

[9] Tomaszek, Tom, "Interview with Grayson Warren Brown," *Modern Liturgy,* Vol. 8, September, 1981, 14-17.

[10] Brown, Grayson Warren, *The Transformative Power of Faith: Stories of Hope, Humor and Healing* (Portland, OR: Pastoral Press, 2014) 237-238.

[11] Yes, "Soulfull" with two L's. Brown borrowed that usage from Fr. Clarence Rivers.

[12] Brown, Grayson Warren, *The Transformative Power of Faith: Stories of Hope, Humor and Healing* (Portland, OR: Pastoral Press, 2014) 235.

[13] Ibid., 236.

[14] Ibid., 236.

[15] Liner notes, *Hymns of a Soulfull People.*

[16] Brown, Grayson Warren, *The Transformative Power of Faith: Stories of Hope, Humor and Healing* (Portland, OR: Pastoral Press, 2014) 238.

[17] Interview with the author, October 5, 2017, by phone from Berkeley, California.

[18] Ibid.

[19] "Your Song of Love" by Bob Fabing, SJ.

[20] Kendzia, Tom and Mary Carol, *Music, Directors, Choir, Songleaders, Accompanists* (Mystic, CT, Twenty-Third Publications, 2003) 34-35.

[21] Interview with the author, September 28, 2015 in Portland, Oregon.

[22] Ibid.

[23] "A Conversation with Raymond P. Bruno," *Billboard,* September 27, 1980.

[24] "New Star on the Horizon," *Billboard,* September 27, 1980.

[25] Interview with the author, September 28, 2015 in Portland, Oregon.

[26] Interview with the author, June 10, 2015, via email from Milwaukee, Wisconsin.

[27] Ibid.

[28] Ibid.

[29] Ibid.

[30] Interview with the author, June 19, 2017 in San Francisco, California.

[31] Interview with the author, June 10, 2015, via email from Milwaukee, Wisconsin.

[32] "NALR Boosts Revenues," *Record World,* November 11, 1978.

Chapter Twelve

"Roll Down the Ages"
OCP and GIA

"History doesn't repeat itself but it does rhyme."
-quote attributed to Mark Twain

"Give us a heart so meek and so lowly.
Give us the courage to enter the song."
-Marty Haugen, from his song, "Gather Us In"

Bob Hurd was back in the recording studio. It had been six long years since he recorded *Bless the Lord,* his 1975 album with FEL Publications that was fraught with production disappointments. Hurd composed the songs on his two FEL collections while a student at the Archdiocese of Los Angeles' Saint John's College in Camarillo, California.[1]

Hurd left the seminary in 1974 to pursue doctoral studies in philosophy at De Paul University in Chicago. He volunteered at a local Catholic Worker house, met Dorothy Day, and entered into meaningful discussions with her about social justice in Church and society. While working on his dissertation, he moved back to Southern California and began teaching at Loyola Marymount University. He participated in campus liturgies and worked part-time as a music minister in a Los Angeles parish. During this busy time of academics and ministry, Hurd's five-year contract with FEL expired. He was now free to start over again as a liturgical composer and relished the opportunity to have greater artistic control over his next project.

Followers of Hurd's music noticed a marked difference between his FEL songs and the music he recorded for his new collection, *Roll Down the Ages.* For his music ministry communities, Hurd began composing songs that were more grounded in liturgy:

> I also began to realize that I should be writing for an assembly—not my individual tenor voice. I began to think critically about melodic range and syncopation. While the center of gravity in pop music is the band or the artist, the center of gravity in worship music is 500 or 800 or 1200 people singing together. Finally, if music is servant of the word and the ritual, rather than an end in itself, one should start with the text, and let the text call forth a melody and chord structure. At the same time, I was growing in theological and liturgical knowledge.[2]

Roll Down the Ages included several Scripture-based songs that were housed in a compelling folk-choral arrangement that was very conducive to the sacred liturgy: "I Am the Light of the World" (composed by Bob's friend Greg Hayakawa); "Alleluia, Lord;"

"I Am the Vine;" and the title song, a call to justice inspired by Amos 5:24 and Dorothy Day. Also included were several settings of official liturgical texts that would eventually be gathered together and published as *Mass of the Incarnate Word*. The recording sessions were held at KSR, a Christian studio on the corner of Hollywood and Vine which, at the time, was a seedy neighborhood. But the sound Hurd and his friends captured was pure gold. The album is credited to "Bob Hurd and Anawim," a Hebrew word meaning "lowly." Bob's encounter with Dorothy Day and his work with the poor in Chicago inspired him to choose that name, and his singers from Loyola Marymount loved it.

Hurd finally had artistic control in the studio but it came at a hefty price from his own pocketbook.

> I went in on a joint venture with Franciscan Communications in Los Angeles. I would produce and pay for the recording, and they would handle the printed music. I realized later that I couldn't keep paying for recordings in this way, so I began to look for a new publisher. My friend, Paul Ford, and I took a trip up to Portland and visited with Owen Alstott at Oregon Catholic Press. I left him a copy of *Roll Down the Ages*. At that time, OCP had a very small staff and was just beginning to grow into the organization it is today. I wasn't really expecting much to come out of this. I tried other publishers without much luck. Eventually, I got a call from Owen saying he'd like to take on *Roll Down the Ages* and feature some of it in their *Music Issue*. 'Oh, and by the way,' said Owen, 'do you have any more music?' By that time, I had written 'In the Breaking of the Bread' and several other songs that became the collection of that name.[3]

Bob Hurd would go on to a very prolific career as a liturgical composer, producing 16 recorded collections with OCP. He was a pioneer in writing bilingual Spanish-English songs with his wife Pia Moriarty and friend Jaime Cortez. Their story will be told in a future book. But his first OCP collection, *In the Breaking of the Bread,* would prove to be groundbreaking for both Hurd and for OCP. The composer had a gift for gentle melody that permeated his new collection on songs like "Shelter Me, O God," "Come Unto Me," "Power of Love," and the title song. This was Scripture-based music that quickly became popular with parishes who were just discovering OCP's *Music Issue* pew resource. Bob toured the country extensively with members of Anawim, bringing excitement and enthusiasm to communities who were hungry for new music.

Oregon Catholic Press

Oregon Catholic Press is unique among liturgical publishers as a non-profit company with an archbishop as its Chairman of the Board of Directors. It had its beginnings in the early 1920s, when the Ku Klux Klan was rampant in Oregon and the persecution of Catholics was one of its main goals. Archbishop Alexander Christie established the Catholic Truth Society—the original name for Oregon Catholic Press. The Society's purpose was to provide Catholics and non-Catholics alike with information about the Church, and the activities of its educational and charitable institutions.

Within two years, the Society was distributing 250,000 pamphlets. The Society became a corporation in 1928 and borrowed funds to acquire the *Catholic Sentinel,* the diocesan newspaper for the state of Oregon.

In 1934, the Catholic Truth Society began publishing *My Sunday Missal,* a small, inexpensive "pamphlet-missal" with each Sunday's liturgy printed in English.

In 1974, the format of the missal was modified to include a better, broader selection of music and its name was changed to *Today's Missal.* The missal gained popularity in 1977 with the initial publication of its companion piece, the annual *Music Issue.*[4]

Today's Missal was OCP's answer to the then popular *Monthly Missalette* produced by J.S. Paluch, a Chicago-based Catholic publisher. "Missalette," a term that Paluch claimed to own, is a Catholic worship aid modeled after the personal missals of the pre-Vatican II era. Published inexpensively in periodical format, missalettes are meant to be replaced after a fixed time.[5] The irony is that OCP was publishing a "pamphlet-missal" in the 1930s, well before the liturgical renewal of the Second Vatican Council. OCP was hoping to recapture a share in this periodical missal market that Paluch dominated. Publisher Owen Alstott and his staff realized that music would be a way to attract parishes and pastors to *Today's Missal.*

The music selection in *Monthly Missalette* was improved considerably when Paluch acquired World Library in 1971. NALR had the popular *Glory & Praise* hymnal but no worship aid distribution. OCP approached NALR and asked for permission to include the songs of the St. Louis Jesuits, Carey Landry, and Michael Joncas in *Music Issue.*

"At first, Ray and Dan were opposed to idea of putting our songs into missalettes," said Erich Sylvester. "They didn't want anything to do with World Library, which was affiliated with Paluch. I eventually convinced them to work with Oregon Catholic Press because, at that time, they were not a competitor. OCP had not yet started publishing any original music. Ray and Dan finally saw the value of that and granted permission to OCP."[6]

Music Issue was certainly appealing, with more than 400 of the songs that American Catholics enjoyed singing: "Sing a New Song;" "Blest Be the Lord;" "Peace Is Flowing like a River;" "On Eagle's Wings," and other contemporary standards, plus a healthy helping of traditional hymns like "Holy God, We Praise Thy Name;" "Come, Holy Ghost," and more. Conveniently sized to be bundled with its companion, *Today's Missal* (with the Order of Mass, readings and propers), *Music Issue* had one other feature that proved irresistible: guitar chords over the measures of all the contemporary songs!

Marie Steiner Philippi, former OCP staffer, traveled the United States extensively, giving music ministry workshops at parishes and conferences. Pastoral musicians were hungry for new songs, and eager to improve their musicianship and their understanding of liturgy. Philippi, a skilled singer and guitarist, led reading sessions and taught guitar technique. At every workshop, a handout, *Music Issue,* was given away free.

Philippi recalls:

> I honestly think that *Music Issue* was like a birthday cake. People were so excited about getting free music at my workshops. They would take it home, share it with their musicians and choirs and, of course, their pastors. The host parish invited all their neighboring parishes and the musicians brought their guitars and sat in front, playing along as we sang through the songs.[7]

Many of these musicians had been on their own, with no guidance, for so many years. Marie took care to teach the finger-picking patterns that the St. Louis Jesuits included in their popular songbooks, and the parish guitarists soaked it up. Pastors noticed increased enthusiasm in their musicians after attending Philippi's workshops. This translated into an assembly that began to sing with more confidence at liturgy. Music directors didn't have to twist their pastors' arms. They were more than happy to switch their pew book from Paluch's *Missalette* to OCP's *Today's Missal* with the handy *Music Issue* supplement that included guitar chords.

Dave Island, former general manager at J.S. Paluch, was there when that company acquired World Library of Sacred Music in 1972. But in the 1980s, Island moved to the Pacific Northwest, and eventually started working for Oregon Catholic Press. He remembers the hard work that Marie Philippi put into promoting *Music Issue*:

> We sent Marie everywhere, to tons of parishes and every convention I could think of. And we gave more personal attention to customers than Paluch did. They had their established way of doing things that worked well for them, and OCP tried to do it better with our 800-number and personal customer service.[8]

Music Issue was successful and helped transform OCP into a major Catholic publisher. And then, without warning, NALR pulled out all its copyrights in 1985. OCP and subscribing parishes were aghast. They couldn't sing the songs of the St. Louis Jesuits anymore!

OCP scrambled to include songs by other composers. Happily, this was when the company was beginning to publish original works by their own artists, including Bob Hurd, Tom Conry, Millie Rieth, Sister Marianne Misetich, and publisher-composer Owen Alstott. OCP also successfully negotiated inclusion of the songs of the Monks of Weston Priory, plus Marty Haugen and David Haas, who were starting to make their mark in the 1980s. Parishes were pleased to discover music by new composers. Still, there was an unanswered question: What was going on with NALR?

As discussed in the previous chapter, NALR hit a critical and financial high point in the late 1970s. Their projected sales were topping $4 million, and the company made plans to reach out to the larger Protestant and secular markets. But by the mid-1980s, NALR was having trouble fulfilling that very basic duty of all music publishers: paying royalties to composers.

What happened?

As nothing official has ever been reported or published on NALR's downturn, and with the principals now deceased, we must rely on research that points to at least two major factors that may have contributed to the company's decline.

For its Phoenix headquarters, NALR was renting an industrial space on 2110 West Peoria Avenue. As income grew into the millions, it made sense for Bruno to invest. Real estate in the Southwest was booming and it seemed like a logical investment. Land was purchased where Bruno would build his new dream home for NALR: a state-of-the-art facility with larger offices, larger warehouse, a recording studio, and an auditorium to feature performances by artists and composers. An architect was hired to design this expensive custom building.

There was plenty of money available for building and construction, due to the United States government's easing of restrictions on lending institutions in the late 1970s. Much of that money ended up in the Southwest, especially in the Phoenix area. "Arizona has been one of the fastest-growing states, and it is still growing more than the country as a whole. But as growth has slowed, a lot of offices and houses have sat waiting for people who never arrived. Moreover, although construction has slowed, some office projects are still rising despite a dearth of renters."[9] Because of this unsustained growth, property values plummeted, along with office rents. Companies caught in this cycle did not have the cash to make payments.

It appears NALR may have been caught in this maelstrom. Their million-dollar income of the 1970s was not happening in the 1980s. Already racked with over-the-top construction expenses, the company had difficulty keeping up their ability to pay royalties. Naturally, this did not sit well with NALR's composers.

Around this time, Dave Island was traveling in the Southwest for OCP, and he stopped by Phoenix to visit NALR. Bruno was delighted to welcome his visitor and, after some gracious pleasantries, Island hinted that he was there to listen and offer support. Bruno admitted that this was a difficult time for him and his company.

"We are interested in keeping you and your work alive," said Island. "How can we help?" Bruno was most concerned with preserving copyright security for his composers, especially the St. Louis Jesuits. This began a series of discussions between NALR and OCP that led to the formation of a joint copyright holding company, New Dawn. The upshot was that, after a three-year absence, "Be Not Afraid," "Sing to the Mountains," and other beloved St. Louis Jesuit songs appeared again in the 1989 *Music Issue*.[10]

The New Dawn arrangement worked for a few years, but NALR's financial troubles continued. Eventually, Bruno had no choice but to enter negotiations that led to OCP's acquisition of NALR in 1994. Ray Bruno passed away a few years later.

"The world was growing," said Ray's son, Bruce Bruno. "The secular world was growing, was moving on in time. And the Church is such a big part of the secular world, if I can say that. In order for the Church to continue, it had to grow with the world."[11]

In the wake of Vatican II, my father started a music publishing company. North American Liturgy Resources began publishing music that was both a pleasure to sing and liturgically based. In the process, he stumbled upon five Saint Louis seminarians he believed could get the Church singing again. My father was a visionary, and he surrounded himself with others who shared his passion for returning the language of prayer to the community.[12]

Ray Bruno's legacy continues today at OCP. Many of the original NALR artists are still composing songs for liturgy and producing recordings that Christians of all denominations can use for prayer and for personal listening enjoyment. OCP published *Glory & Praise, Second Edition* as a hardbound hymnal in 1997. It included many songs of the original *Glory & Praise* series that have stood the test of time, as well as new music composed by the company's considerable roster of composers. In 2015, *Glory & Praise, Third Edition* was released with new songs composed since the previous edition, plus Mass settings that utilized the official Mass texts of the revised *Roman Missal, Third Typical Edition.*

In 1982, OCP released a new periodical missal, *Breaking Bread,* combining the contents of *Today's Missal* and *Music Issue* into one convenient annual edition. Originally published with only scripural citations, the complete Sunday readings were included in the 2000 decade. *Breaking Bread* became OCP's flagship publication.

The influential composers of England's Saint Thomas More Group were introduced to America by OCP in 1986. These composers included Christopher Walker, Bernadette Farrell, Paul Inwood, Ernest Sands, Stephen Dean, Peter Jones, Anne Quigley, and more. Their music was hailed for its compositional sophistication, liturgical sensibility, and congregational accessibility.

The year 1989 saw the publication of *Flor y Canto,* a comprehensive hymnal of Spanish and bilingual Spanish-English music that included more than 700 songs and psalm settings plus six Mass settings composed by the leading Hispanic composers from around the world, including Cesáreo Gabaráin, Carlos Rosas, Mary Frances Reza, Pedro Rubalcava, and Juan A. Espinosa. Ten years later, OCP published *Spirit & Song,* a collection of youth-oriented songs for both liturgy and youth events, featuring music by many of the recognized youth ministry composers of the day, including Tom Booth, Tom Tomaszek, Steve Angrisano, Trevor Thomson, Jesse Manibusan and Ken Canedo.

Marty Haugen

Born in 1950, Marty Haugen, the son of Milton and Gwen Haugen, hails from Eagan, Minnesota. Marty came from a musical family. His mother sang in her college choir and played piano, and his grandfather played violin. "I took piano lessons when I was six, played trombone in high school band, and picked up the guitar—like a lot of my generation—after we heard The Beatles. My dad didn't want me to have a guitar, but my uncle gave me one, so my dad couldn't refuse it. I took up violin and organ in high school."[13]

Haugen went to college as a music major but changed his focus after his freshman year, opting instead for a degree in psychology from Luther College in Decorah, Iowa. But he continued his involvement in music, continuing with piano lessons and playing tunable percussion in the college band. "I was fortunate to have played a string instrument, a brass instrument, percussion, organ, piano, and guitar at various times. That was a real help for me."[14]

For a time, Haugen considered ordained ministry. He was working as an orderly in a hospital, and the chaplain there suggested the young musician look for a job in a local Catholic church:

> I said, 'I don't know anything about Catholic liturgy,' and he said, 'These days, nobody does. You'll feel right at home.' And he was right. After the Second Vatican Council, Roman Catholics were asking questions like, 'What does it mean to gather? How do we sing the psalms? How do we sing when we go to Communion?' I think the Spirit moves through questions and discussions and struggles like those.

> Growing up in the Lutheran Church, I knew and loved the psalms, but only as prayer texts and spoken texts, not sung. The first Sunday I came to the Catholic Church; we were instructed to sing the psalm—interactively! The response of the people was tentative and much of the music at the time had not yet developed its later sophistication as composers improved their craft.

> And so, I experimented right off the bat. As most musicians do, I approached composition from the standpoint of music, and I tried to make the text work with the music. But I realized very quickly that was a distortion of the role of music in worship. What the church taught me was how critically important it is that music support the Word. Learning to compose for the text—to make the music support the text—was a long process for me.[15]

Haugen started composing psalm settings and other Scripture-based songs for Saint Bonaventure Catholic Church in Bloomington, Minnesota. He recorded his work and hand-engraved the arrangements. All he needed was a publisher.

"I went to the very first NPM in Scranton, Pennsylvania in 1978," Haugen remembered.

> I went to the NALR booth and they had the St. Louis Jesuits, Carey Landry, and the Dameans. And it was clear that they didn't need me at all. Then I saw another booth for Pastoral Arts Associates of North America. They were publishing the music of Joe Wise, whom I have always admired. And I talked to Dan Onley, and he said, 'Okay, give me your master tape, and give me your manuscripts and I'll see what I can do.'[16]

Onley pressed an album from Haugen's master tape and printed his hand-engraved manuscripts as is, and . . . it never went anywhere! "But it got my foot in the door. Later on, other publishers started noticing me." Fellow Minnesota composer Michael

Joncas also noticed Haugen, and invited him to serve as accompanist for a conference in Chicago where Joncas was presenting.

> That's where I did 'Gather Us In,' which at that point wasn't recorded or published. GIA noticed it, and then told me that they'd like me to send music for publication. And when they said they'd publish things, I had a contingent. I said, 'I'll go with you if you buy my music from Pastoral Arts Associates.' Because, I had just done a second album, *With Open Hands,* with PAA, which had 'We Remember,' 'We Are Many Parts,' 'Be with Me Lord,' and 'Canticle of the Sun.' So, there were songs in there that I didn't want to have disappear.[17]

The Chicago publisher agreed and released *With Open Hands* as a GIA collection in 1980. Those songs have since become standards in Catholic liturgy, but it was Haugen's Mass setting that established him as a premier composer.

> My second parish was Saint Timothy in Blaine, Minnesota. When it came time for the Triduum, they didn't celebrate together but divvied up the days: one choir took Holy Thursday, another choir took Good Friday, and another choir took the Easter Vigil. And I suggested that we needed to celebrate the Triduum liturgies together. I composed *Mass of Creation* so it would work across styles.[18]

Published in 1984 by GIA, *Mass of Creation* was groundbreaking in that it allowed guitarists and organists to work together on the same piece of music. Haugen studied the compositional techniques utilized by Richard Proulx and Bernard Huijbers, and he employed a Dorian mode that is characteristic of Appalachian folk music. Lastly, Haugen utilized the priest-friendly key of G minor that encouraged presiders to sing the Preface and the related dialogue prayers with confidence. *Mass of Creation* became the most widely used Mass setting of the late 20th century. It has since been published for use in Lutheran liturgy, and was recently revised with the official Mass text of the new *Roman Missal, Third Typical Edition.*

Haugen worked for nine years on a master's degree in pastoral studies from the University of Saint Thomas in Minnesota, in the midst of his full-time parish work. He went on to compose more than 400 songs and 47 recorded collections published by GIA, Augsburg Press and other publishers. One of his most beloved songs is a setting of the iconic Psalm 23. At first, he hesitated to compose the song. "There are so many wonderful settings of that text," said Haugen.

> I kept stumbling over the word 'shepherd' because I had never personally known someone who was a shepherd, and I had never spent time with shepherds. My wife suggested that it could be a verb, and that sort of became my way into the psalm. I could understand being shepherded by someone, and I imagined God is shepherding us, leading, guiding us. It was a helpful image.[19]

"Shepherd Me, O God" became a much-loved hymn, sung at funerals and other occasions of consolation. Its poetry touches the hearts of Christians across all denominations. Haugen and his family now worship at Mayflower United Church of Christ in Minneapolis.

GIA Publications

The main story of this book has focused on NALR, with a respectful nod toward FEL, World Library Publications (WLP), and OCP. But it is also important to acknowledge the influential role played by the Gregorian Institute of America, more popularly known as GIA.

Clifford Bennet founded the Gregorian Institute of America on December 8, 1941, at Sacred Heart Church in Pittsburgh, Pennsylvania. His focused goal was the instruction of Catholic church musicians. He established annual summer sessions and a Catholic choirmasters correspondence course, "a 110-lesson home-study program, which was completed by 900 musicians during its first decade of existence."[20] The Institute began publishing in the late 1940s, and its English language Holy Week participation cards sold in the millions. After the Second Vatican Council, Bennett and his staff confronted the shifting tides that emerged from the sudden popularity of folk music in the liturgy.

> Clifford Bennett and the Gregorian Institute of America faced the challenges of the vernacular liturgy with energy and enthusiasm. There were two widespread developments which Bennett chose not to join: the publishing of guitar music and of missalettes. After the Council, Bennett entered into an agreement with Carl Fischer, Inc., of Chicago in order to become distributor for Gregorian Institute editions. Edward Harris was manager at Carl Fischer with whom the agreement was negotiated. When eventually Bennett told of his plans to sell, Harris collected all of his assets and purchased the Gregorian Institute of America on November 1, 1967.
>
> In 1967, Gregorian Institute of America moved from Toledo to Chicago with Ed Harris and Robert Batastini at the helm. Gregorian Institute of America was changed to GIA.[21]

GIA distinguished itself as a major hymnal publisher. Observing the success of World Library's *People's Mass Book*, GIA released *Worship* in 1971, edited by Robert Batastini. *Worship* was a good start, but GIA hit a critical homerun in 1975 with the release of *Worship II*, edited once again by Robert Batastini, plus noted composer Richard Proulx. It featured 19 Gelineau psalms and 313 hymns by such traditional composers as Fred Kaan, Sydney Carter, Isaac Watts, and Charles Wesley, together with contemporary classical composers Jan Bender, Calvin Hampton, and Alexander Peloquin. The lofty goals of *Worship II* were eloquently expressed in the edition's Preface:

> The Roman Catholic Church has its own sacred music tradition, but the tradition does not include a long history of singing in the English language.

Musicians and liturgists have long expressed need for a Roman Catholic hymnal that is theologically sound, embraces the fullness of liturgical practice with all its options, and respects the hymnological traditions of those commonly referred to as "protestant" hymnals.[22]

The new edition received favorable reviews:

A reading of the first lines shows that much is new, off the beaten path and practical... The accompaniments to many of these hymns command attention, for their fresh approach presents a welcome relief from the usual block harmonies. Their lines are very fluid, the number of voices vary, and a few have independent accompaniments. Early American folk hymn collections have been tapped and a few folk hymns of the present era added. (J. Vincent Higginson).[23]

GIA's founder Clifford Bennett chose not to participate in the publication of guitar-based songs, but the company's later success with Marty Haugen, David Haas, Michael Joncas, Gary Daigle and other contemporary composers necessitated the inclusion of modern songs in a third edition of *Worship* in 1986. A companion volume entitled *Gather* was released in 1988, giving even more focus to contemporary hymnody. Interestingly, NALR was part of this endeavor.

David Haas

David Haas, the son of Bob and Joan Haas of Bridgeport, Michigan, was born in 1957. His father, a pianist and organist, managed a music store, and during the Korean Conflict, served in the Army as a chaplain's assistant, providing music for Catholic, Protestant and Jewish services. His mother was a public-school music teacher for Kindergarten through 12th grade, and she was David's choir director at Bridgeport High School during his four years there. She also taught chant and voice to a community of cloistered Carmelite nuns in Traverse City, Michigan. Both parents taught private music lessons, and were involved over the years as directors of local musicals. David's older brother Jeffrey is a musician and actor, and his sister Colleen has a doctorate in ethnomusicology and teaches at various universities.

I come from a musical family. We have pianos in my house. Our church was just across this field from our house. Dad played the organ and mom directed the choir. We had this incredible relationship between music making at home and also doing church music. I have so many memories of parties in our house where we all gathered around the piano and sang.[24]

In college, Haas studied piano and voice, and thought he might want to be a music teacher. "My major interest in those days was musical theater," David remembered. "I wanted to do musicals and even opera. I was involved in a lot of them."[25] Haas was noticed in theater circles, and after an audition, he was offered the part of Tony in a touring production of *West Side Story*. But there was one problem. On the very week that Haas was offered the role, he was preparing to enter the seminary! "I had a week of sleepless nights as I struggled with what I should do. I decided to turn the part down because I really wanted to pursue seminary studies for the priesthood."[26]

And so, Haas moved to Saint Paul, Minnesota.

> The diocese sent me to Saint John Vianney Seminary. I was there for two and a half years, and that is when I started to write songs. I put together my own recording—just my friends at the seminary and other college friends. We just went in there and did it. About three or four months after that came out, I got a phone call from Michael Joncas. I was at the college seminary, Saint John Vianney, and Michael was across the street at the Saint Paul Seminary, which was the major seminary. He was just about to be ordained a deacon, right after *On Eagle's Wings* came out. He said, 'I just heard your LP that you did (*I Am Yours Today*). I like it very much and we should get together and have lunch.' About a year after that, I left the seminary.

> I still was working on finishing my degree, in both music and theology. During that time, I met Marty Haugen who was doing music at a parish in a suburb of Minneapolis. I went to Mass there and introduced myself.

Eventually, Haas, Haugen and Joncas got together to share music and ideas.

> That started our partnership. We really didn't know it was one at the time, but we started to bring music that we were writing to each other. We started doing workshops and concerts together. The first one was in 1982 at my parish, Saint Thomas Aquinas, where I invited the two of them. I never dreamed that this would be something that would continue all these years later.

> It was a win-win in the sense that we did things together. I remember I conducted a choir for one of Michael's records and I would sing some solos on Marty's. Marty produced my very first recording that I did with GIA. We supported each other and helped each other with arrangements sometimes, and so forth. At the same time, we had our individual endeavors that we wanted to do as composers. It really was wonderful. Sometimes it would be two out of the three.[27]

Haas has composed several songs that are considered as classics in the contemporary Catholic repertoire, including "Blest Are They."

> The parish where I worked, Saint Thomas Aquinas [in Saint Paul Park, Minnesota] had a commitment to a Catholic Charities program. My friend Barbara from the parish served there. I was so moved by that sense of dignity that she gave to the street people. I remember getting home to my apartment after that, and the song came pouring out of me in about ten minutes. The line in the refrain, 'blessed are you, holy are you,' was from watching how Barbara gave of herself. God is with you in the suffering that you have. That's what makes you blessed.[28]

Haas' beloved song "You Are Mine" came from personal experience.

> I was going through a very, very difficult and painful time in my life, when I felt a lot of isolation, a lot of abandonment. I felt very broken; very depressed. I was angry at God and angry at myself. The song came raging out of me in seven minutes. I didn't play it for anybody for about a year and a half because, number one, it felt too personal and, number two, no one could possibly be feeling what I was feeling. That incredible sense of the pain you're going through; no one could possibly relate to this.

> Do not be afraid, I am with you.
> I have called you each by name.
> Come and follow me, I will bring you home;
> I love you and you are mine.
> ©1991, GIA Publications

"You Are Mine" was released on the second volume of Haas' *Who Calls You by Name* collection, which sprang from his involvement with the North American Forum on the Catechumenate, a lay-run organization founded in 1981 to provide formation and support to dioceses and parishes in the emerging ministry of the Rite of Christian Initiation for Adults. Haas was inspired to compose music for such RCIA rites as the Rite of Acceptance, the Rite of Election, the Scrutinies, the Blessing of Water at the Easter Vigil, and the Renewal of Baptismal Promises. These collections of RCIA music also debuted some of Haas' most enduring songs, including "Deep Within," and "We Are Called."

Over the years, David Haas has been very active as a workshop presenter and keynote speaker at parishes and conferences around the world. He has recorded more than 50 collections of liturgical music, and is the author of several books, including: *Prayers Before an Awesome God (The Psalms for Teenagers); Music and the Mass;* and *Welcome, Faithful Presence: A Week of Praying the Hours with Henri Nouwen.* Haas has received numerous awards and recognitions, including a Doctor of Humane Letters Honorary Degree from the University of Portland. But of all his many accomplishments, Haas is probably most grateful for Music Ministry Alive, a program of liturgy formation for young people that he founded in 1999.

> When I was young I had the benefit of having adults in my life who took an interest in my talent and wanted to nurture it. They saw the diamond in the rough, so to speak, and wanted to pull that out. I went to a lot of high school music camps where we lived in the dorms on a campus and learned from the college professors about band and choir, and we got a taste of college life. And we had the opportunity to work with other musicians who were of the same level.

> So, I had this idea: Wouldn't it be cool if we had a church music camp for high school teens and early college-age students? I started talking with the director of youth ministry of my archdiocese, and we got it organized. That first summer we had 95 kids, not just from Minnesota but from 14 other

states, too. I asked my composer and liturgy friends to be on the faculty, for a terribly small stipend. And I went to the publishers. OCP, WLP and, especially, GIA provided free music because we had no funds for this program. We incorporated and kept it going, and had our 19th year in 2017.

To date, about 2,500 young people have gone through the program from around the world.[29]

Most composers and pastoral musicians will attest to how the spark for their involvement in liturgical music was kindled in their youth. Through Music Ministry Alive, David Haas has inspired a new generation to take up the call to serve the Church as musicians, composers, and leaders.[30]

•■•

By the mid-1980s, Catholic liturgical music was moving on from the explosive growth of the 1970s. So much had happened since that fateful stormy day when Ray Bruno decided to move NALR out west to Phoenix. So many new composers emerged who gave the Church so much new music. The raw enthusiasm of the Folk Mass era had matured and blossomed. Hard lessons were learned as the composers and the publishers took note of both the triumphs and the trials of those who had climbed the mountain before them.

Catholic liturgical music had most definitely become an "industry," but it is on the parish level, in the pews, where this music really matters, as the People of God gather to listen to the Word and be nourished by the Bread of Life.

---

[1] For more on Bob Hurd's early career, see Canedo, Ken, *Keep the Fire Burning: The Folk Mass Revolution* (Portland, OR: Pastoral Press, 2009) 124-125.

[2] Ibid.

[3] Ibid.

[4] Reddy, Jon, "Today's Liturgy Celebrates 25 Years!" *Today's Liturgy,* Vol. 25, No. 1, Advent-Christmas-Epiphany 2003 (21-22).

[5] "The issue of missalettes had become a divisive one. Even though most American Catholics know participation aids through the use of some form of missalette or mimeographed sheets, liturgists had been strong in their opposition to their use. [Omer] Westendorf reported caustically, 'The state of hymnals is pitifully weak, and the state of missalettes is disgracefully flourishing... The very concept of throw-away hymns and throw-away scriptures tends to reinforce their feelings of insecurity, of unending changes of a faith in a permanent state of flux.'" See Boccardi, SM, STD, Bro. Donald, *The History of American Catholic Hymnals Since Vatican II,* (Chicago, IL: GIA Publications, Inc., 2001) 59. Westendorf quote from his essay, "The State of Catholic Hymnody," *The Hymn:* 28, no. 2, (April 1977) 54.

[6] Interview with the author, June 19, 2017 in San Francisco, California.

[7] Interview with the author, October 13, 2017 in Portland, Oregon.

[8] Interview with the author, October 4, 2017 in Vancouver, Washington.

[9] Norris, Floyd, "Market Place; Valley National: Different Opinions," *New York Times,* February 21, 1989.

[10] Interview with the author, October 4, 2017 in Vancouver, Washington.

[11] Interview with the author, February 10, 2007 in Beaverton, Oregon.

[12] Gale, Mike, editor, *The St. Louis Jesuits: Thirty Years* (Portland, OR, Oregon Catholic Press, 2006) 71.

[13] Interview with the author, October 20, 2017, by phone from Eagan, Minnesota.

[14] Ibid.

[15] Brink, Emily R., "Minister of the Word-Through Music: An Interview with Marty Haugen," *Reformed Worship,* No. 58, December 2000 (32).

[16] Interview with the author, October 20, 2017, by phone from Eagan, Minnesota.

[17] Ibid.

[18] Ibid.

[19] Ibid.

[20] Boccardi, SM, STD, Bro. Donald, *The History of American Catholic Hymnals Since Vatican II,* (Chicago, IL: GIA Publications, Inc., 2001) 3.

[21] Boccardi, SM, STD, Bro. Donald, *The History of American Catholic Hymnals Since Vatican II,* (Chicago, IL: GIA Publications, Inc., 2001) 36.

[22] Preface to *Worship II,* (Chicago, IL: GIA Publications, Inc., 1975).

[23] J. Vincent Higginson, review of *Worship II* in *The Hymn* 42, no. 2, (April 1991) 12. As cited in Boccardi, SM, STD, Bro. Donald, *The History of American Catholic Hymnals Since Vatican II,* (Chicago, IL: GIA Publications, Inc., 2001) 66.

[24] "A Conversation with David Haas," GIA video, May 4, 2107. https://www.youtube.com/watch?v=Z6KWppQB-nE

[25] Interview with the author, December 14, 2017, via email.

[26] Ibid.

[27] "A Conversation with David Haas," GIA video.

[28] Ibid.

[29] Interview with the author, September 9, 2017, in Portland, Oregon.

[30] Similar programs such as One Bread, One Cup at Saint Meinrad School of Theology and the Steubenville conferences would also help nurture the faith and spirituality of young Catholics going into the new millennium.

Epilogue

"Give us faith, Lord,
when the mountain's too high."
-Dan Schutte[1]

National Association of Pastoral Musicians' (NPM) conventions are always a celebration. Pastoral musicians look forward to the annual gathering to rekindle friendships, learn about the liturgy, sing through packets of octavos, and pray the Eucharist with the full, conscious, and active participation encouraged by the Second Vatican Council. The 2001 convention in Washington, DC, was even more special. Not only was it NPM's silver anniversary, but also a bittersweet farewell celebration for Father Virgil Funk, who was retiring as president of the influential organization he founded in 1977 with literally nothing more than faith and vision.

There were many tributes to Funk that week, and many musical celebrations of NPM's 25 years. Perhaps the most memorable was the musical retrospective produced by OCP.

> Near the end of the program the commentator announced, "We'd now like to call on stage a group of men who've contributed enormously to the prayerful worship of Christian churches throughout the world. They haven't sung together on stage for nearly twenty years. Ladies and gentlemen, please welcome the St. Louis Jesuits."

> The response was immediate and unmistakable. People rose to their feet as Bob Dufford, John Foley, Roc O'Connor and Dan Schutte stepped onto the stage. The joyful, driving musical introduction to "City of God" began. For the next four minutes, hundreds of voices raised the roof of the Omni-Shoreham ballroom with song. Many, including the Jesuits, sang with tears in their eyes.[2]

I was playing bass in that small group of musicians, conducted by composer Gerard Chiusano. We had rehearsed a few days beforehand and were sworn to secrecy about the surprise appearance of the St. Louis Jesuits. I was behind the Jesuits on that stage and could only see the backs of their heads, but there was no mistaking the shock and then the joy of the faces of the audience in front of us. As we all sang "Let us build the City of God, may our tears be turned into dancing," I, too, had trouble keeping my composure as my eyes welled up in tears.

Roc, Dan, John and Bob were amazed by the response to their appearance at that NPM event. For several months, via emails, phone calls, and in person over coffee, they discussed what it all meant. In 2003, they got together in San Francisco to share new songs they had been working on. They made the decision to go into the studio one more time to record songs of hope and encouragement.

NALR was long gone, so the composers regrouped in Portland, Oregon, in 2005 at Dead Aunt Thelma's, OCP's recording studio. True to the way they originally worked when they were young men, the St. Louis Jesuits were creating new music during the summertime. One happy event of their reunion was having Tim Manion, who left the group in 1983, join them in Portland for four days. The others in the group had not seen Tim, who now lives in Phoenix, for over twenty years.[3]

In the 1970s, the St. Louis Jesuits were the troubadours of their generation—Baby Boomers who were either in college, or just beginning their careers and families. In *Morning Light,* the St. Louis Jesuits are walking gently with their listeners as friends who understand the mystery of life and death.

The St. Louis Jesuits were back! Their new songs, all written for liturgy, once again touched many hearts with the composers' sincere faith and love for God.

In this book, I have used the mountain as a central metaphor, based on Dan Schutte's "Sing a New Song," that so joyously offers praise to God from the mountaintops. The journey up that mountain has not always been pretty, but it's a eucharistic pilgrimage that has hopefully strengthened and unified us along the way.

I wrote these concluding remarks on the Second Sunday of Advent and that morning during liturgy I was struck by the First Reading from the prophet Isaiah.

> A voice cries out: In the desert prepare the way of the Lord!
> Make straight in the wasteland a highway for our God!
> Every valley shall be filled in,
> every mountain and hill shall be made low;
> the rugged land shall be made a plain,
> the rough country, a broad valley.
> Then the glory of the Lord shall be revealed.[4]

I suddenly realized the flaw of my central metaphor. If we consider the journey to God as a mountain, a challenge that must be climbed, then God will forever be out of reach. But God comes to us! God meets us where we are, with all our flaws and imperfections. There is no mountain; every mountain shall be made low. It falls upon us to clear the highway and allow God to enter our hearts. Then the glory of the Lord shall be revealed.

Don't get me wrong. God is indeed transcendent and infinite, and I love music such as Gregorian chant that expresses that divine mystery so eloquently. In fact, I need chant and polyphony and the pipe organ to help keep me theologically balanced in my understanding of God as I pray the liturgy. But, as someone who grew up in the post-Conciliar era, the contemporary expression of liturgical music equally moves me to celebrate the God who has walked in our shoes, who was tempted to sin like I am, and who experienced grief, loss, and joy. In other words, this daring experiment of using secular-based music to worship the transcendent God has opened up a fresh hearing of God's Word for today's society.

The ongoing discussion on styles and music in Catholic liturgy will continue to be politicized unless efforts are made by everyone to learn where each side is coming from. In my books, I have tried to share the story of contemporary Catholic music. I can only pray that those who champion chant and traditional hymnody will also share their stories, and that lovers of contemporary music will read them, so that "we, who are nourished by the Body and Blood of your Son and filled with his Holy Spirit may become one body, one spirit in Christ."[5]

---

[1] "Give Us Faith, Lord," © 2004 by Dan Schutte. Published by OCP Publications.

[1] Gale, Mike, editor, *The St. Louis Jesuits: Thirty Years* (Portland, OR, Oregon Catholic Press, 2006) 144-145.

[2] Ibid., 152.

[3] Isaiah 40:3-5.

[4] Eucharistic Prayer III.